The Driftwood Shrine

The Driftwood Shrine

Discovering Zen in American Poetry

∽

John Gendo Wolff, Sensei

THE DRIFTWOOD SHRINE
Discovering Zen in American Poetry
John Gendo Wolff

Designed by Karma Yönten Gyatso

Published by
The Sumeru Press Inc.
PO Box 2089, Richmond Hill, ON
Canada L4E 1A3

LIBRARY AND ARCHIVES CANADA CATALOGUING IN PUBLICATION

Wolff, John Gendo, 1958-, author
    The driftwood shrine : discovering Zen in American
poetry / John Gendo Wolff, Sensei.

Includes index.
ISBN 978-1-896559-28-5 (paperback)

    1. Zen Buddhism in literature. 2. American poetry--History
and criticism. 3. American literature--Buddhist influences.
I. Title.

PS310.B83W65 2016   811'.009382943927   C2016-903704-5

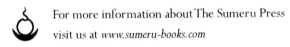

For more information about The Sumeru Press
visit us at *www.sumeru-books.com*

Contents

Foreword

Zen is a practice that goes beyond words and letters and points directly to the human heart. So why have so many Zen masters written so many words about Zen? When used properly, words can expand one's life. An important part of Zen practice is to learn to use live words in contrast to dead words. Live words arise from one's experience and dead words are based on concepts and abstractions.

When a Zen master utters a live word to his disciple, the intent is to jolt the listener into a high level of spiritual awakening or to help him or her to evolve along the path of awakening. Poetry can have the same effect. Poetry pushes the boundaries of one's imagination and one's grip on a safe, conventional life. Even nursery rhymes can have that affect. As a child, I remember reciting "Row, row, row your boat gently down the stream. Merrily, merrily, merrily, merrily. Life is but a dream." Then I wondered what was real if life is nothing but a dream. Even now, as I reflect on these simple phrases, they are still quite profound.

Chinese Master Wumon praised Master Yangshan by saying "He preached a dream in a dream." Pointing to a peony in the garden, master Nanquan Puyuan said, "People these days see these flowers as if in a dream." My late master, Taizan Maezumi, often said to me while pointing around, "Life is a dream." Makes me wonder if "Row, Row, Row Your Boat" was written by a Zen master.

In *The Driftwood Shrine*, John Gendo Wolff is using American poetry to illustrate profound principles of Zen. He shows us how the poets open their hearts and go beyond words and letters to point us to the heart of all humans. As the American poet and Zen practitioner Gary Snyder wrote: "Meditation looks inward, poetry holds forth. One is private, the other is out in the world. One enters the moment, the other shares it. But in practice it is never entirely clear which is doing which."

As Gendo illustrates, Zen meditation turns poetry while being simultaneously turned by poetry. He presents a wide range of American poems and finds treasures hidden in all of them. Gendo carefully examines each poem as if it were a Zen koan (the sayings used by Zen Masters to awaken the cloudy minds of their students). *By slowly and meticulously walking on the tightrope of words, the meaning behind the words is revealed.*

The poems are the finger pointing at the moon. As we penetrate beyond their apparent meanings, the clouds of delusion lift and the moon shines brightly. As a writer and teacher of literature and poetry and as a Zen teacher, Gendo Wolff has shed new important light on these poems and has given them a life beyond life.

The William Carlos Williams poem "The Red Wheelbarrow" is so simple in appearance that its depth is unexpected.

> so much depends
> upon
>
> a red wheel
> barrow
>
> glazed with rain
> water
>
> beside the white
> chickens.

As Gendo writes, if you deeply reflect on this poem it "will force you to question your common sense thinking, your cloud of delusive thought. The harder you try to give common sense answers to a question like *What exactly 'depends upon' a red wheelbarrow?* the faster your common sense disappears in a haze of uncertainty. That experience changes the nature of the question. Penetrating deeper into it, you may notice yourself asking something simpler, something more direct, like *What is the red wheelbarrow?*"

Zen Master Yuean Shanguo said to a monk, "Xizhong made a cart whose wheels had a hundred spokes. Take both front and rear parts away and remove the axle then what will it be?" Take away all concepts of the red wheel barrow and experience it directly. Then, what is it? Like Zen Master Yuean, Gendo invites us to look beyond appearances.

In "Facing West from California's Shores," Walt Whitman writes, "Inquiring, tireless, seeking what is yet unfound." Whitman sounds like a Zen student. The famous essay, "Fukanzazengi," by Zen Master Dogen starts, "After exhaustively searching, the Way is perfect and all pervading." This exhaustive searching is an essential part of finding what is yet unknown. As Gendo comments on this poem, "it's a little step *backward* that brings us all the way home, all the way back to our original place. That little step backward is to just not know. This is not the same as being ignorant or going into a trance or hiding in denial. Not knowing is vast like the sky or vast like the Pacific Ocean."

In Zen we say "not-knowing is most intimate." When we think we know something, we fossilize it and cease to seek further. The Zen teacher Gendo encourages us to keep seeking beyond seeking, and the literature teacher Gendo encourages us to use these wonderful poems to seek what is yet unfound.

Gerry Shishin Wick, Roshi
Great Mountain Zen Center
Berthoud, CO

Preface

Bringing *The Driftwood Shrine* into print is the culmination of my 35-year period of fascination with the history of the intersection of Buddhism and American poetry. The seminal moment of this interest occurred in the late 1970s when I was a student at the University of Cincinnati. At that time, I thought I was going to be an archaeologist, a specialist of extinct people and exotic places. What I didn't know then was that there are archaeologies of the self that lie unknown until brought into the light of day by a good teacher.

For me, one of those teachers was Professor Michael Atkinson. He became, in a sense, the Dr. Leakey to my psychological and academic Olduvai. Michael was a brilliant teacher who not only galvanized my interest in literature but graciously read my juvenile poetry and encouraged me to continue writing. I took all of his courses, including *Eastern Thought and American Literature*, a course that taught me about the mental and artistic spaces which Asian spiritual traditions and American poetry had been sharing for two centuries. I learned about the fascinating parallels between the cosmic "I" of Whitman's "Song of Myself" and the touchstone of Vedantic Hinduism, *Bhagavad-Gita*; about the surprisingly large number of American poets who had taken an interest in Buddhism, sometimes becoming converts; and I learned how the poetry of writers as diverse as Henry David Thoreau and W.S. Merwin, or Jack Kerouac and T.S. Eliot could be so brilliantly illuminated by Buddhist notions of impermanence, emptiness, attachment, and nirvana. These experiences made up the watershed that changed the course of my life.

I looked deeply into myself, questioning what it was I was doing with my life. And Michael supported this search as much as he had encouraged me to keep on writing. A Buddhist himself, trained primarily in the Vipassana tradition, he was in a perfect position to guide me and some of his other interested students in our beginning meditation practice. Sitting with him, I eventually started to realize that my future was not going to be about archaeology in the literal sense, but in the sense that I would be unearthing the self, using the tools of poetry and Zen.

Graduate school followed, and many years later, I too was an English professor.

I took every opportunity to acquaint my literature students with a few basic tenets of both Hinduism and Buddhism—ideas that I hoped would help them understand the unique and passionate interest that so many American poets have had in Buddhist ideas. And, when I eventually earned a sabbatical, I used my time to read much more extensively about the influence of Eastern thought on American writers. It was during that sabbatical that I came across an anecdote that not only captured the nature of my long-standing interest in this particular East-West confluence, but illustrated the rapt enthusiasm with which the American Transcendentalists had sought out books on Hinduism, Buddhism, Taoism, and Confucianism in the early decades of the 19th century.

According to the story, Henry David Thoreau received a "royal gift" of forty-four books on Eastern religions from his English friend Thomas Cholmondeley. They were exceptionally rare books which Thoreau cherished for the rest of his life. Thoreau shared the news of their arrival as one might, he said, share news "of the birth of a child." He then proceeded to shelve these treasures in a bookcase that he had made out of driftwood from the Concord River, an act by which, as the biographer Franklin Sanborn put it, Thoreau had given "Oriental wisdom an Occidental shrine."[1]

One might think that Thoreau's "driftwood shrine" was an unfitting container for the sophisticated wisdom of a tradition like Buddhism. To me, however, that wisdom was all the more at home in its simple, worn, and worldly wooden case. Zen is always about what is readily at hand—a broom, a coffee cup, a window box full of weeds. "Grasses and trees, fences and walls, tiles and pebbles," wrote the great master Eihei Dogen (1200–1253) , "carry out buddha work." The naked immediacy, the humble acceptance of things as they are, the acknowledgement that all things and beings are a reflection of ultimate reality—all these are common to the nature of driftwood and Dharma alike. They are qualities that can be discovered now in the poetry of Americans—many, many of whom have been influenced by the light of the Buddha-dharma.

Among such writers are, as I mentioned, the Transcendentalists and their contemporary Walt Whitman. They had little accurate knowledge of Buddhism in those days, but their explorations opened the way for further, deeper digging. Ralph Waldo Emerson's early investigations of Eastern thought had had the effect of a stone thrown into a pool of still water, and the ripples have been expanding ever since. Encompassing not only all of the Transcendentalists (including skeptics like Melville and Hawthorne), those ripples reached outward and onward—to John Greenleaf Whittier, John Hay, Vachel Lindsay, John Gould Fletcher—and, in the modernist period, a host of experimental poets like William Carlos Williams, Gertrude Stein, H.D., Ezra Pound, Amy Lowell, Wallace Stevens, and T.S. Eliot, all of whom had meaningful "conversations" with the East. Often, the influence of Eastern thought on these writers was the result of their admiration of *haiku*, the Japanese form of poetry that

so economically embodies Zen insight. But there were other cases, in which the relationship with Buddhism was deeply personal. The pain of the personal crisis that T.
S. Eliot endured while composing "The Waste Land," for example, had driven him to
consider conversion.

As access to more—and more accurate—information about Buddhism became
available in the 20th century, those small Emersonian ripples grew even wider in the
American literary pond. A great many of the Beat Generation's writers—such as
Diane Di Prima, Anne Waldman, Allen Ginsberg, Jack Kerouac, and Philip Whalen—
took a personal, not just literary, interest in Buddhism, as did their contemporaries
Kenneth Rexroth and Gary Snyder. In the late 20th and early 21st centuries, some
of our greatest writers, like W.S. Merwin, Richard Wright, Alice Walker, Peter
Matthiessen, bell hooks, *and too many others to mention*, have all connected to Buddhist
practice. Many in this grocery list are converts, and at least three (Snyder, Whalen,
and Matthiessen) became Zen priests. At least two (Whalen and Matthiessen) were
fully authorized to *teach* the Dharma as Zen masters—no small spiritual attainment
by any means.

I too eventually became a priest, but it took a long time to get there. For many
years, I practiced Zen meditation on my own. Partly this was because I had a family
and a livelihood to make, and partly it was because of the scarcity of qualified Zen
teachers in the intermountain west where I lived. I contented myself with a home
practice in the basement of a rented house in Pocatello, Idaho, until one bright, cold
winter morning, my view of the world changed. Sitting in meditation, I suddenly looked up, and the objects on the altar were no longer as they once were. Or
they were more than what I thought they were. My eyes lit upon the Buddha image,
the candle, the flowers, and the smoldering incense, and back again, over and over,
checking to see that I was actually seeing what I thought I was seeing. Each time my
gaze lit on an object, it was none other than myself that I saw. The normal subject-
object duality that characterizes consciousness had disappeared.

The experience is certainly not unique to me, but it is the kind of thing that gal-
vanizes interest and makes commitment, born of gratitude, possible. It would still be
a long journey from that moment to the one in which I found my teacher, but I knew
with absolute certainty that I would never retreat from the path.

At some point about fifteen years ago, I travelled with a friend to Indiana, sent
there by a former teacher, to study with Susan Myoyu Andersen, Roshi. I arrived at
dusk on a beautiful spring evening and was standing on the porch when she arrived.
The trees seemed to slide into a dark silence as she silently floated from the car to the
house. She seemed transfixed. I didn't want to interrupt her deeply concentrated state.
But as she floated up the steps of the porch, I suddenly blurted out an introduction.
She immediately turned and gave me a radiant smile. Even in the dim light, her blue

eyes glinted. "It's nice to meet you," she said, and then she was gone into the house.

I cannot convey the full range of spiritual gifts of trust, harmony, joy, and gratitude that I received from Myoyu Roshi, but will just acknowledge here a single one: acceptance of myself. One of the ways that Myoyu Roshi taught me (and others) to accept myself was to be a stickler for the details of zendo etiquette—of the formal proceedings of ceremony, chanting, eating, and other business of monastery life— the legacy of her 20-year discipleship with Taizan Maezumi, Roshi, founder of the Zen Center of Los Angeles. Because her sangha was relatively small, everyone covered multiple temple "positions," which afforded me a great deal of practical experience, almost always under Myoyu Roshi's direct supervision. I made lots of "mistakes." With all the emphasis on form, it was inevitable that I would feel embarrassed when I rang the bell at the wrong time, or in the wrong way, or not at all. Or when I forgot to bow or to hold my hands "just so." The feeling of embarrassment was rooted in the mistaken idea that the formal behaviors of the zendo were born of a militaristic discipline that was somehow necessary for awakening. With time, however, I learned that following form is not militaristic at all. It requires mindful attention, of course, but Myoyu Roshi never judged the quality of her students by the number of successes or failures they had in following form.

Following form was not just Zen boot camp behavior, but a matter of practicing the traditional "perfections," or *paramitas*, especially *kshanti-paramita* (patience) and *virya-paramita* (effort). On the one hand, we were to work hard and put forth our best effort; on the other hand, any "mistake" in our form was to be met with patience and equanimity—never embarrassment or shame. Once that was clear, I made many fewer "mistakes," and I began to value tradition in a way that often seems at odds with the white, male, left-leaning professor-identity to which I clung.

More importantly, I learned that tradition, when viewed in the right way, is not a constraint, but the means by which our real personalities are revealed. When our habits of projecting an idealized personality are temporarily suppressed by the tradition of form, a more genuine, authentic, and unique self appears in its place. We can't help it. We are who we are. A roomful of people who are eating in exactly the same way, from identical sets of bowls, and in accord with a traditional set of manual maneuvers may at first appear as a choreographed ballet. But closer inspection reveals that each person is blossoming out of the soil of tradition in a way that is unique to them. At times, this phenomenon of psychological transparency is so pronounced that each person's thoughts and feelings come into sharp relief. At the same time, because each person is connected to every other by the same formal tradition, their unique qualities intermingle and harmonize, producing an atmosphere of serenity and reassurance. In that kind of environment, one more readily sees just how reasonable and natural it is to accept who we are, just as we are.

As my training with Myoyu Roshi evolved, I was eventually asked to start giving Dharma talks. It's one thing to teach college classes, to stand up every day in front of strangers and assert some version of the truth and hope you make it through the day. It is quite another to give a Dharma talk with your teacher in the room. But because of what the tradition and Myoyu had given me, I knew better (if not perfectly) how to respond to any feelings of self-consciousness that might have arisen. I also knew that I could always put my trust in the fact that I was no one other than the person I was, no matter what I did or failed to do in passing on the teaching.

So I chose to do something a little unusual: I talked about poetry. Not "Zen" poetry, but western (usually non-religious) poetry whose authors had been influenced to one degree or another by Zen. Being able to come at the Dharma in a new and unusual way, using the idiom of American poetry, was just a part of who I was.

I started with a talk about William Carlos Williams' poem "The Red Wheelbarrow." A talk centered on a poem by Wallace Stevens soon followed. Later, I gave a talk focused on Ezra Pound's "In a Station of the Metro," and later still I gave a talk on a poem by Walt Whitman. It began to be clear that a body of work was forming itself. I had begun to cobble together a collection of American poems that, in their uniquely western form, were like Thoreau's driftwood bookcase: beautiful structures made of English words that sheltered and focused the gentle light of the Buddha's wisdom.

Talks and essays, however, are two very different kinds of communication. In the former, I could tailor my talks to touch on the things that I perceived to be the "needs" of students whom I knew personally. But the twelve essays that comprise *The Driftwood Shrine: Discovering Zen in American Poetry* had to be written for a great many people that I will probably never know—people for whom the practice of Zen may be unfamiliar. That means that some explanation of the form of this book is in order.

Following Classic Koan Collection Structure

Overall, *The Driftwood Shrine* has been structured to reflect the koan literature that has comprised the bulk of my training in Zen. *Koans*—often translated as "public cases"—model certain perspectives on Buddhist realization. While there are many variations, a koan typically begins with what is sometimes called a "pointer"—a brief introduction that metaphorically contextualizes the koan. The koan itself comes next, usually in the form of a bit of recorded dialogue between a Zen master and a student. An extended commentary, aimed at helping students realize the meaning of the koan follows. And, finally, that commentary is capped off by a poem that summarizes the main spirit of the koan.

The structure of *The Driftwood Shrine* follows in the footsteps of this tradition, except that it uses poems as the "public cases" that help us develop the depth and clarity of our spiritual insight. Thus, you will find a pointer at the beginning of each essay, and I have closed each essay with a *waka*-style poem. The number of words in the lines follows a 5-7-5-7-7 pattern. This structure makes *The Driftwood Shrine*, I believe, the first full-length book of Dharma teachings to use poems in this way.

As you might expect, the poetry that you will find here engages with the nature and practice of mystical insight, the fundamental experience of Zen practice. Whether it is Gary Snyder's down-to-earth riprap, Walt Whitman's blue vistas, William Carlos Williams' glimpse of a red wheelbarrow, or Emily Dickinson's deeply introspective revelations, the poets that together comprise this series of shrines have connections—some faint, some fully committed, most somewhere in between—to the tenets or practice of Buddhism.

That said, none of the poems you see here will stridently promulgate "Zen ideas." They do not cheaply cash-in on Buddhist imagery or come off as polemical, preachy, or didactic. On the contrary, the influence of Zen on these poets, like ink in water, or the scent of flowers in the air, is suffused throughout their work. These poems naturally and organically *embody*, rather than vainly trumpet, the nature of spiritual practice and inquiry. This is just as it should be.

One realistically could identify a thousand poets whose work enshrines the Buddha-dharma and would be worthy of inclusion in this book. I regret that I could not include Diane Di Prima's "No Problem Party Poem," or Anne Waldman's "Make-up on Empty Space," or an excerpt from Jack Kerouac's *The Scripture of the Golden Eternity* or *Mexico City Blues*. I wish I could have delved into Kenneth Rexroth, Bob Kaufman, Theodore Roethke, Lorine Niedecker, Nathaniel Tarn, or bell hooks, but the fact is that space and energy are always limited. I make no claim to inclusiveness, therefore; I have tried to be alert to opportunities to welcome a variety of voices from different times and places, but mostly the poems you see here are just ones that I have enjoyed for a long time.

The essays are arranged in four sections. **The Path**, which treats the topics of conversion and the Zen path itself; **Impermanence, Suffering, and No-Self**, the traditional Buddhist *trilaksana*, or "Three Marks of Existence," that characterize the conditioned nature of our lives; **Seeing Straight**, which treats a variety of common life experiences from the perspective of Zen practice; and, finally, **Endless Practice**—essays that are intended as reminders that Zen is a long-term endeavor.

These organizational and thematic aspects of the book, however, will likely be more useful in retrospect. You should feel free to read the essays in any order that pleases you, letting the poems themselves inspire your path through the book. It is important, however, to read the poems *aloud*. It is hard to explain, and impossible to over-emphasize, that the brilliance of the poem-jewel is never fully appreciated until it is polished by the living breath. It isn't hard to do this if you read aloud with the feeling that you will never do it again. Unless you are willing to let go of all of the caked-on make-up of the "self" that each of us projects onto the world, a poem read aloud will not leave your mouth sounding like a poem—and some part of its meaning will be lost.

Other kinds of words must be treated differently, of course. These would include traditional Zen and Buddhist terms. For terms that are commonly seen in both their Sanskrit and Pali versions (such as *anatman* and *anatta*, for example), I've made an arbitrary decision to use the Sanskrit. I have also tried to ensure that, if you have not seen these words and phrases before, you can understand them through context, and I frequently provide brief definitions immediately after these special terms.

The names of Chinese masters that have to come to us in the Western Zen tradition have almost always been rendered in Japanese. Where possible, I have tried to restore these names to the Romanized version of Chinese using the pinyin system, except that (as is common in non-scholarly works) the diacritical marks that would indicate the tones used in spoken Chinese have been omitted.

My hope is that if you are new to Zen, *The Driftwood Shrine* will inspire you to practice. For those who are already practicing, I hope that *The Driftwood Shrine* will provide a fresh perspective on familiar terrain and encourage deeper practice. To that end, I have endeavored to include some significant challenges in this book so that even advanced practitioners will find something worth their while. Recognizing that I may have failed in these ambitions, however, I would simply point out that the poetry in *The Driftwood Shrine* is, all by itself, worthy of your reading time. If you yearn for a spiritual authenticity and originality in an age of reckless and irresponsible speech, you need only look at the poems that have been growing like weeds in our own backyard for nearly two centuries. The Dharma gleams in these poems in both subtle and profound ways.

We may never know exactly how it is that poetry and Zen do so much for us, but surely, as the great American poet William Carlos Williams put it, "Men die miserably every day for lack of what is found there." You will be no less perfect, whole, and complete if you never read another word of *The Driftwood Shrine*. But if you feel the lack that Williams was writing about, please don't wait for the inevitable, unhappy outcome. Just turn the page.

1   Christy, Arthur. *The Orient in American Transcendentalism: A Study of Emerson, Thoreau, and Alcott*. New York: Octagon Books, 1963. Print. 47.

Author's Acknowledgements

This book would never have come into being if I had not had the great fortune, as a student at the University of Cincinnati many years ago, to study with Dr. Michael Atkinson, now emeritus Professor of English and Comparative Literature. His intellect, sensitivity, and breadth of mind was both inspiring and encouraging. In particular, his course *Eastern Thought and American Literature* opened my eyes to the many American writers who have been influenced by Eastern religious and philosophical thought, and this has remained a life-long interest. I have always felt a deep gratitude for Michael's kindness, his creative spirit, his humor, and his open, honest character.

I also wish to thank several others.

My agent and long-time friend Kenneth Wapner provided remarkably persuasive, insightful, passionate advice in helping me shape this book. In an era when most of us need to prod others for attention, it was refreshing to know that Kenny would often be the one to place a call or to write to me with helpful thoughts and encouragement.

John Negru has been everything that a writer could possibly wish for in a publisher: a gracious and encouraging advisor, a creative entrepreneur with a wonderful sense of humor, and a wise, compassionate advocate of the Dharma.

Seán Henne and Michael Nagle, my faculty colleagues, have also supported my writing with frequent words of encouragement and selfless interest. Seán provided invaluable assistance in helping to improve the overall unity of the book.

The West Shore Community College Board of Trustees approved a sabbatical leave during which I conducted research on the lives of American poets whose work has been influenced by Eastern thought.

My wife of over thirty years, Tandy Sturgeon (a superb writer herself) provided a number of excellent critiques of my early drafts, and cooked food and brought it to my study so that I could continue to work without interruption.

Finally, I wish to extend my great thanks to Susan Myoyu Andersen, Roshi, my teacher of many years, for all that she has done for me. Her steadfast patience and seemingly endless reserves of wisdom, compassion, and creativity kept me afloat through all the difficult—and all the wonderful—years of training. There is no time when I think about all that she has done for me that I am not overcome by waves of gratitude. My debt to her can truly never be repaid.

Copyright Acknowledgements

number 36.21.1. Photo credit: Seiji Shirono, National Research Institute for Cultural Properties, Tokyo.

Tiananmen photo: https://commons.wikimedia.org/wiki/File:Tiananmen_1901.jpg.

For my teachers
Dr. Michael Atkinson
and
Susan Myoyu Andersen, Roshi

The Path

Course Correction

Jones Very's "The Lost"

An ancient map on edgeless paper, a path drawn with invisible ink.
Following the compass of ten-thousand hands, how do you find the Way?

The Lost

The fairest day that ever yet has shone
Will be when thou the day within shalt see;
The fairest rose that ever yet has blown,
When thou the flower thou lookest on shalt be;
But thou art far away among Time's toys;
Thyself the day thou lookest for in them,
Thyself the flower that now thine eye enjoys;
But wilted now thou hang'st upon thy stem;
The bird thou hearest on the budding tree
Thou hast made sing with thy forgotten voice;
But when it swells again to melody,
The song is thine in which thou wilt rejoice;
And thou new risen 'midst these wonders live,
That now to them dost all thy substance give.

(1839)

One might think it odd to begin a book about poetry and Zen with a sonnet by an evangelical, 19th century Christian. Yet "The Lost" by Jones Very (1813–1880) has always spoken to me as a "Zen" poem. Mellifluous and kind, its gentle lines are formed of twilight speech, a message born of night admixed with day. And what better reason could there be to let Very's bird sing here, at the front door of *The Driftwood Shrine*, than that the Dharma sun is rising, bright, within you? His poem is the perfect invitation to do what you must to get "unlost," to find your way across the territories of "Time's toys." It is like one of the ancient Chinese stories, or *koans*, that have been used for centuries as objects of meditation in Zen—a koan that suggests the path to liberation can be found in a bird that sings with your "forgotten voice."

You can trace a family resemblance between "The Lost" and "Brahma," a poem by the Transcendentalist writer Ralph Waldo Emerson, which relies on the same kind of rhetorical balance and paradox to convey the nature of union with the divine:

> If the red slayer think he slays,
>   Or if the slain think he is slain,
> They know not well the subtle ways
>   I keep, and pass, and turn again.
>
> Far or forgot to me is near;
>   Shadow and sunlight are the same;
> The vanished gods to me appear;
>   And one to me are shame and fame.
>
> They reckon ill who leave me out;
>   When me they fly, I am the wings;
> I am the doubter and the doubt,
>   I am the hymn the Brahmin sings.
>
> The strong gods pine for my abode,
>   And pine in vain the sacred Seven;
> But thou, meek lover of the good!
>   Find me, and turn thy back on heaven.

"Brahma" is clearly indebted to the Hindu Upanishads and to *The Bhagavad-Gita*, works of Eastern thought that Emerson adored, and which he often mined for his embellishments. Yet for all that—and perhaps because of it—"Brahma" is to "The Lost" as smoke is to fire. Emerson wrote, you might say, from the perspective of one who studied the mystical experience, but Very wrote from the experience itself. He was the real deal.

So real, in fact, that, at the peak of his creative and spiritual powers (1838 to 1839), Very hardly needed Emerson, Thoreau, or any of the other Transcendentalists to provide the very Eastern sense of union with the divine that can be seen in his poems. True, Very would probably not have been blind to Emerson's enthusiastic embrace of Hindu thought. Nor would he have missed the fact that his first and perhaps closest friend among the Transcendentalists, Elizabeth Peabody, just happened to be the first person to translate Buddhist scripture into English. But Very's spiritual inspirations had originated within him, not as a response to the Eastern literary predilections of his peers. He believed—quite literally—that the Holy Ghost had inhabited him, causing him to undergo a transformational conversion experience that echoed elements of Hindu incarnation and Buddhist oneness.

Like Very, you too can empty body and mind of its preoccupations with external forms of pleasure. No longer lost "among Time's toys," you too can discover that "The fairest day that ever yet has shone" is not beyond you, but within you.

Lost Among Time's Toys

What does it mean to be "far away," lost "among Time's toys"?

Toys, of course, are playthings. They encourage imagination and awareness in children. But the toys in our poem are not connected to brain development or social skills. They are the material things and social positions that, consciously or unconsciously, we hope will shore up a sense of ourselves as firm, fixed, and enduring.

Our toys come to us as houses, cars, clothes, food, friendships, loves, and pleasant weather. One by one, each toy becomes the object of attachment. And one by one our toys disappear, or change, or *we* change and our suffering begins. Our toys are ephemeral, unlasting. Yet we go on, year after year, persisting in a belief that a fixed state of happiness can be wrangled from the *unfixed* phenomena of the world. We think—and we are encouraged by numerous social mores to think—that the accumulation of material wealth and the control of our outward circumstances will produce a future contentment. We think, in other words, that happiness is *derivative*.

On one level, it's easy to accept the fact that people, animals, insects, skyscrapers, airplanes, and plutonium—indeed, the Earth itself—will not be here forever. On another level, however, admitting that we are spiritually lost can cause so much painful bewilderment that we may prefer to continue the dream than to wake up. I am often amazed at how much suffering we humans are willing to endure out of a fear of what the alternative may come to.

There was a time I remember when I looked down from the top of my high-rise college dormitory, working up the nerve to jump. I had alienated my friends, neglected my studies, and had not a clue as to how the whole business of living was supposed to be conducted. In the distance, the thin, barely discernable line of the Ohio River gleamed in the late afternoon light; a lonely barge stilled itself on its brightness. Below, the traffic of the city honked and roared, while nameless thousands of people walked, talked, and thought through their world as though it were an easily navigated path. But for me, life had become inexplicably agonizing. I was lost. To be lost like that, lost within your own life, is to have no business anywhere else. It is to be alone. And so, all alone, I had fallen into a kind of blackness that consumed my days. I was too young to manage such overwhelming darkness and too far gone into despair to imagine how things could ever be different.

I hoisted myself up on the edge of the building and looked straight down. Suddenly, the loud metal of the streets, the hot clanging of cars and busses went silent. I judged the distance and knew there could be only one result. I drew in a breath then, very slowly, very evenly and prepared to let myself fall. I was in a state of almost thrilled relief and joy. And then I hesitated. In that brief moment, the brink of my coming release suddenly became the brink of terror. I backed away from the edge.

Over the next several days, I reread a couple of books about Zen. I knew something about how to meditate, but I had not been disciplined about it. But now, with my rooftop view of life and death lingering in my mind, I set off into a daily sitting routine. Almost immediately, I found myself back in the swing of college life—books and friends and beer. Within one semester, I went from probationary status to the Dean's list. I wasn't a sensational college student, nor a sensational student of Zen by any means, but I had come to a crucial turning point in my life.

It's unfortunate that so many of us go on pursuing life's traditional game-plan, even though we know it's delusional. We stay lost, almost on purpose, stubbornly postponing life. This can be illustrated by an experience I once had while walking in a woods—a woods where I had walked several times before. On this particular day, I came upon a pleasant grove of birch trees. It was a very inviting spot. I lay down in the long, soft grass and dozed in the mottled light until it was late in the afternoon. When I woke up, I set out for home, heading first for a landmark that I'd used many times before to guide me to the road: an old, broken-down, barbed-wire fence. After a while, however, I knew I had passed it up; it was nowhere to be seen. So I kept walking. And walking. And walking.

Suddenly, the heavy canopy overhead began to give way, and a bright spot appeared through the trees ahead. I felt relief at the prospect that I had come back to the road in spite of not having found the fence. I walked toward the bright spot, expecting to come stomping out onto the road, but what I came into instead was the very same grove of birch trees where I had napped twenty minutes earlier. The hair on the back of my neck stood up. I had walked in a circle!

I started out for home once again. Now, however, I walked at a faster pace, trying to make up lost time. I tried to neutralize unpleasant thoughts about being lost, telling myself that I had missed the fence because I had been momentarily distracted. By and by, however, the eerie sensation that things weren't right came over me again.

I had somehow missed the line of the old fence a second time and stood once more in stunned bewilderment in the same little cluster of birch trees. A cold river of goose-bumps trickled down my neck. It was as though I had been cursed to never leave the enchanted forest. The hopeful, purposeful path that I had laid out for myself had left me wandering in circles.

And so it goes in life overall. You pursue the same doomed course, even though the expected landmarks of progress fail to appear. It is all about our tendency to re-peat the same mistake, again and again, for lack of any alternatives. It is all about ratio-nalizing purposes and failures, weaving a fabric of self-deceit, desperately defending a path we are expected to follow until we die.

But there comes a point when your head "hangst upon thy stem" and "wilted," you have to face the startling fact that "the fairest day that ever yet has shone" is not where you thought it was. It is, as Very tells us, within.

The Turning Point

When I realized that I had walked in a circle, not just once, but twice, I was so flab-bergasted that I had to sit down. Back in the tall grass, I didn't move for a long, long time. I did not know which way to turn. I reviewed everything I had done, the steps that I had taken, the landmarks that I had expected to use, but there was no explanation and no one to blame but myself. With a dollop of wounded male pride, I swallowed the inescapable conclusion: I was totally lost. It was only when I really started to look around at my surroundings, to take in the details of the woods around me, to appreciate the actuality of my life at just that moment, that I was able to find my way home. I had had to slow everything down so that I could scrutinize each moment of experience as it ticked by.

That effort to slow down and pay attention is the same kind of effort that you put forth when quieting the mind in the practice of *zazen*, or seated meditation. Zen pacifies the ego's frantic search for its own substantiation, making it possible to notice that walking in a circle is not the path to happiness but the path of suffering. When you notice this, you can't help but want to do something to correct your course.

In Buddhist terms, this turning point is not merely a matter of deciding to take up the practice of Zen. To recognize *the reality of suffering* is the first step along the Way. In fact, it is the *only* step you ever take in Zen practice. To sit zazen is not merely a matter of becoming tranquil, but is to enter a realm of day-by-day and moment-by-moment conversion, gradually deepening your realization of the nature of suffering and the cessation of suffering. From that turning point onward, your work is to discover, as Jones Very tells us, that "The fairest rose that ever yet has blown" is not somewhere down the road of wealth, social position, and power, but here, now, in the form of the flower of your very own life.

The turning point is a spiritual proposition nicely echoed by an element of the English sonnet form which Very chose for "The Lost." It is known as the *volta*. The volta, appropriately enough, is usually referred to as "the turn," and it represents a shift in perspective, one that usually resolves a dilemma that was laid out at the beginning of the poem. It is, in some sense, a course correction. In Very's poem, you are presented with the idea that, while the "fairest day" is within you, you do not see it because you are all caught up in your grasping after ephemeral things, "Time's toys."

The Buddha himself was no exception to being lost "among Time's toys." Living a life of luxury in his father's palace was one form of being lost; another was in following the futile practice of asceticism, undergoing painful austerities in the mistaken belief that they would eventually make him happy. It wasn't until he came to his own turning point—the moment in which he nearly died of starvation—that he was open to re-evaluating his life.

In a famous depiction of this moment, filmmaker Bernardo Bertolucci showed Siddhartha seated in meditation along the banks of a river, nearly dead from fasting. Just then, a boat drifted across Siddhartha's gaze upon the river. On the boat, a musician was speaking to his pupil. "If you tighten the string too much," explained the teacher, "it will snap. If you leave it too slack, it will not play."[2] When Siddhartha heard these words he suddenly realized that his chosen path—just like the path he had followed in his father's palace—was a goal-oriented system of rationalizations that could never bring about happiness. He realized that he was still lost. "Wilted" like Very's flower, he had to change course once again. This time he vowed to sit beneath the Bo tree until he realized the truth about his life.

Lost for Good

From the Zen perspective, to be wilted with disappointment is not such a bad thing. To see your life as a foolish pursuit of an impossible reality is to already have done two significant things: you have acknowledged the reality of suffering, the Buddha's First Noble Truth, and you have entered onto the first part of the Buddha's Noble Eight-Fold Path to liberation: Right View. While there are many facets to understanding what it means to have the Right View, it is fundamentally about acknowledging the reality that life is characterized by suffering—unless you do something about it.

Doing something about it is not a step to be taken lightly. I have learned to be a bit suspicious of beginners who say that they want to throw themselves into Zen practice. Until they have a grip on the real nature of suffering, it is easy to persist in goal-oriented thinking, believing that 100 percent immersion in Zen will lead to happiness in the same way that people think cars and money and green lawns will lead to it.

When these eager beavers don't "get" happiness from Zen practice, they feel cheated, robbed, foolish, or even angry. They often blame the teacher for their failure to find what they're looking for. The real problem, though, is that they have not yet recognized that they are truly—*and irrevocably*—lost.

It is especially important, therefore, to take it slow in the beginning and let your teacher provide some context for practice. When one engages in any kind of spiritual practice with as much intensity and resolve as Very did, it is possible to induce insights that are so powerful that they cannot be easily reconciled with the mundane and frustrating realities of daily life. It's all sweetness and light until you drop the eggs. To help close the gap between your initial insights into the nature of being lost, therefore, it is essential that you rely on an experienced teacher who can help you avoid clinging to your discoveries.

This is one thing that Jones Very did not do—to his detriment. For all his passion and genuine insight, he became obsessed with the conviction that his body, speech, and mind were divinity made manifest. Attached to his own conversion experience, he no longer viewed himself as lost. His vision overran its context. In his arrogance, he behaved as though he were above social conventions, accusing strangers of hypocrisy and insisting, almost violently at times, that all before him submit their wills to God. Many—perhaps most—of the people who saw these behaviors declared that he must be insane. Eventually, he was committed to an asylum. When he emerged two months later, he was a broken man.

We might take a lesson from Very's misfortunes by undertaking the path of Zen with a certain amount of care and caution. This is not at all because meditation or the practice of Buddhism can in any way lead to mental illness—they most assuredly do not. It is because the Zen path, being a path of transformation, is rich with the potential for self-deceit. Trying to correct your course in life without a teacher, therefore, will generally have one inevitable outcome: going off course.

It's true that being lost is no fun. And it's true that you must admit that you are lost before you can correct your course. But once you've done that, it is very easy to imagine that you're done, that you've found the "answer." You then become attached to the value of your turning point, believing that everything you do is inherently "good" or "correct." The fact is, however, that we all need more than a single glimpse of the delusive nature of "Time's toys" to overcome the conditioning that would have us walk in circles. The role of the teacher, therefore, is first to make us aware that we are lost, and then—often to our surprise—to help us see that we must stay that way if we want our practice to really work.

To be *lost*—in the deepest possible sense—is to recognize that your situation is not just a temporary condition. It *is* the very nature of your life, and it's not going to change.

Day after day, I come to the turning point of realizing just how lost I am. That is my practice. I hope that one day you are that lost too! When you are as lost as I am, perhaps you will write a book to help me get home. I hope you do! When you understand what being lost is all about—and it's never what you think it is—it's like re-orienting a map of the wilderness so that it can be correlated to the landscape. The effect is instantaneous, marvelous, liberating! You swiftly move from a state of deflated hopelessness to one of rejoicing. And this map, the map of the Dharma, is large, really large. In fact, it is so large that no one has ever found the edge of it. Now you might think that that sounds pretty impractical, but you can also think of the infinite size of this map as a great relief. The infinite size of the map means that everything in our lives *is* the Buddha, *is* the Buddha's teaching, and the means of realizing that teaching. When you have deeply penetrated what I am saying, then you will want to lift up everything with both hands because everything will be these Three Treasures.

The Bird Thou Hearest

All this talk about the turning point is just to explain why it is that no one was ever born as a Buddhist. Every Buddhist is a convert to the Buddha Way, even Siddhartha. This is because every Buddhist is a person who has had to realize and accept the First Noble Truth—that life is characterized by suffering. You have to know that this Truth applies to you. If you think you can hold some part of your life sacrosanct, or that you can put it somewhere beyond the reach of The First Noble Truth, then you're not yet at that fundamental turning point where Zen practice can really do its best work. But if you realize there's no escape from being lost, then the words of teachers and buddhas become powerful, surging with deep meaning throughout your whole life. When you hear the Dharma preached, it will seem like something you heard once a long time ago, or it will seem as though it were intended specifically for you. If you hear it deeply and clearly enough, you will hear it and see it everywhere.

You will understand in a most intimate way what Very means when he writes, "the bird thou hearest on the budding tree / Thou hast made sing with thy forgotten voice." These are perhaps my two favorite lines of poetry ever! How perfectly they express the essential reality!

When you really penetrate into the meaning of these lines, then you'll understand that the forest in which you're lost goes on forever. It covers the whole world. The forest is within you and without you; it is you. It's not possible to be lost in the woods if everything in the world is woods. It is not possible to be missing anything if everything is you.

We live in a world of forests and mountains, green lawns, jobs, and children. But each of these things is, in essence, you. Take them apart, and take the parts apart, and keep doing that until all you have is atoms, until all you have is the space between atoms, and then everything is the woods, the bird, the sky, the cup, and the table. Everything is the sound of your forgotten voice.

If you think about it, this means that the teaching is being continuously preached all the time, by all things and beings. Including you. There is nothing you have to achieve or attain, nothing that you have to go find. To realize that you already have everything—that you already have the voice that made the bird sing, and that it has been singing all along *whether you heard it or not*—is to actualize the potential of the whole universe. Jones Very might have called this God. Not God in the sense of the personal creator-deity, but in the sense of absolute reality, the omnipresent fact of all existence.

Of course, words like "God" and "omnipresence" are easily spoken, but they are very hard to conceive in any kind of imaginative or visual sense. So if you want to experience God as Very did, or as millions of Buddhists have, then begin by remembering that your forgotten voice is not something "within" you like a soul, or outside of you like your clothes; it is not limited to the body or mind. There is only one, true, all-pervading nature. It would be enough to just say "nature," but we say "true nature" because it must be realized.

So you can call your true nature "God" or you can call it the Treasury of the True Dharma Eye. But these are just words used by sentient beings to describe the nature of the Buddha's life, which sentient beings do not really know. What it is that sentient beings do not know is just this life as it is. When you are lost, you also do not know just this life as it is, but when you are truly lost, and lost for good, then you just don't know. Do you see the difference? It means that the Buddha is himself completely and hopelessly lost, endlessly walking in a circle. It also means that his walking in a circle is your salvation.

Still, the Buddha too must be emancipated. Someone must bring him out of the woods, someone must help him, or realize him. If you do not save the Buddha, then he cannot save you. Joining him face to face among time's ephemeral toys, realizing his unborn and undying nature, you will see "Treasures," "Dharma Eyes," and "buddhas," and your own "true nature." You will also see nothing at all. It is all just the song of the diamond bird and the music of the iron flute. It extends forever in the ten directions.

Life after life, moment after moment, just come to this turning point, and all will be well.

> Dodging cars on the freeway,
> Stepping forward wherever the cane has tapped,
> Buddha wanders alone, completely lost.
> If you think you understand, tell me:
> What's the turning point of the wind?

∾

1   Bertolucci, Bernardo. *Little Buddha*. 1993. Film.

Earth-Touching Gesture

Gary Snyder's "Riprap"

The Path is made of many words, but just one word covers the whole Earth.
What is that word? To find out, the left hand of the floor and the right hand of the broom
must meet. It is really beneath the dignity of a Buddha to behave like this, but how can you
save all sentient beings if the floor is not clean?

Riprap

Lay down these words
Before your mind like rocks.
      placed solid, by hands
In choice of place, set
Before the body of the mind
      in space and time:
Solidity of bark, leaf, or wall
      riprap of things:
Cobble of milky way,
      straying planets,
These poems, people,
      lost ponies with
Dragging saddles—
      and rocky sure-foot trails.
The worlds like an endless
      four-dimensional
Game of *Go*.
      ants and pebbles
In the thin loam, each rock a word
      a creek-washed stone
Granite: ingrained

with torment of fire and weight
Crystal and sediment linked hot
all change, in thoughts,
As well as things.

(1959)

Many years ago, when I was a freshman at the University of Michigan, I attended a poetry reading by Gary Snyder (1930–). I went to the reading not knowing who Snyder was. I left knowing much more about myself. And I knew that, wherever I was headed in life, I wanted poetry to be with me on the journey. Part of the reason for the extraordinary experience that I had that night was that Snyder read his work while "conducting" it with his right hand. His hand bobbed and caressed the air beside him, emphasizing the organic rhythms and the flowing changes of tone in his poetry. Mesmerized, I savored poem after poem, gorging myself on the lilting cadences. I didn't even notice that ninety minutes had passed, making the reading a good half hour longer than most. But everyone in the auditorium felt as I did: if there were more words coming, they'd be gratefully accepted.

Over the subsequent decades, I have learned that a great many poets (myself included), "conduct" their writing lives. This "conducting" is not usually a part of a public performance as it was on that night forty years ago when I heard Snyder read. Rather, this conducting takes the form of journal entry directives that give a poet a certain charge. In one way or another, these directives help poets to stay on the poet-path, focused, fresh, and alive. "Riprap" is one such directive written as a poem. It is a case of Snyder giving himself his life's charge: to build the "rocky sure-foot trails" of his poems with words "placed solid."

Our practice of Zen should be guided by a similar charge: to be ever mindful, present, and engaged with our environment. Mind and world meeting with sufficient intensity create the "fire and weight" that fuses together the diverse, interdependent actualities of our lives. Word and action, mind and place, wisdom and the great earth—these are the "crystal and sediment linked hot" that actualize our awakening in the real world. Connecting with that world, again and again, like a lightning bolt touching the earth, we might say that our "charge" is to practice the transformative act by which the whole world is conducted into our lives and our whole lives back again into the whole world. To borrow a famous phrase from another American poet (Walt Whitman), it is to "sing the body electric."

This notion of touching the earth is an important archetype in Buddhism, and the subject of countless numbers of paintings and statues of Shakyamuni Buddha. In these images, the Buddha's hands are in the *bhumisparsha mudra*, or "earth-touching gesture." His left hand rests palm upward in his lap, symbolizing *prajna wisdom*, the wisdom that is present when we are sitting in *zazen*, or seated meditation. The fingertips of his right hand extend out over his knee to gently touch the ground, symbolically connecting prajna to the wisdom of the Earth—to nature. This positioning of Shakyamuni's hands recalls the moment when he requested the Earth to bear witness to his unsurpassed spiritual authority. The Earth had seen all of Shakyamuni's previous lives—lives that had been spent in the whole-hearted pursuit of supreme, perfect, unsurpassable enlightenment. When the earth roared out, "I bear witness!" Mara, the demon of delusion, and

Bhumisparsa or "Earth Witness" mudra.
Photo by John Gendo Wolff.

all of his minions fled, leaving Shakyamuni free to enter nirvana.

Touching the earth not only suggests that enlightenment is natural, but that the human mind's most natural condition is that of wisdom and compassion. In spite of its naturalness, however, touching the earth is a life-long practice of grounding (to continue our play with the electricity metaphor) our insight. Manifesting your understanding of the Dharma in the real world, through physical action, speech, and the development of compassion—or through the functions of body, speech, and mind—helps prevents the accidental discharge of your natural power in uncontrolled ways. (If you want to know more about this, you may want to read the first essay in this book which explains how the mystic poet Jones Very failed to recognize the importance of grounding his own penetrating realization.) Like riprap—the layer of rocks spread on mountain trails to help horses keep their footing—our practice is a layered work of many years that enables our progress along the path to enlightenment.

Body Riprap

Snyder is not a poet who writes recommendations for others' lives. He did what he charged himself to do, and he lived in service of that charge long before he wrote about it in "Riprap." His life is chock full of forthright physical engagement. He's made his way through life as a sailor, a fire lookout, a lumberman, and a watershed activist with direct, personal knowledge of the mountains and rivers he seeks to protect. In his youth, he worked as part of a forest service trail crew, putting down riprap in the Sierra Nevada, undoubtedly a physically challenging form of labor.

But Snyder combined this hard physical labor with the labor of speech and mind as well. He stopped at nothing to gain access to books about Japan, trying to learn the language, even when obstructed by government officials who were bent on destroying the lives of alleged communists. When he was finally allowed a passport, he wasted no time in becoming a Zen monastic, learning Japanese whenever he was not serving the temple and working its grounds. He never lacked the courage to just let go of doubt and single-mindedly touch the earth wherever he could, doing what he called "the real work." That kind of dedication, it seems to me, is moved by a great moral imperative to so harmonize wisdom and compassion through life and work that he began to resonate like a bell held close to another bell that is ringing in the earth.

The Buddha too, of course, stopped at nothing to fulfill the path. It would be hard to think of anyone who endured greater austerities, sacrifices, and betrayals to earned authority than those endured by Shakyamuni. From the day he left his life of luxury in his father's palace, until the day of his enlightenment, he followed a brutally punishing road to salvation. Even after he adopted a more moderate form of practice, it was still a physically austere, and relatively uncompromising discipline. It should come as no surprise that he is considered the archetype of unwavering commitment to the path, a complete body-and-soul commitment, that allowed him to be truly grounded.

If you too really want to enact the miracle of grounding yourself, therefore, you first have to get in contact with the earth. One really simple way of doing this is to follow Snyder's example: work with your body. That is why *samu*, the work period that is a daily part of Zen practice, has been such a long-standing tradition. When you engage with a broom, a saw, or a sponge, as part of samu, you do so in order to wear away your coarser attachments—starting with your view of samu as "work."

The stony word "work" is often understood only in opposition to words like "play" or "leisure." If you haphazardly place these words together "before the body of the mind," then the act of, say, sweeping the floor, can appear to be a form of drudgery, rather than the enlightening activity it might be. It may be helpful in this context to remember that the word samu is usually translated as "to wipe clean," a handy bit of riprap that may help you recognize that you are not just "working," but wiping away your attachments.

When I lived in China, I would sometimes hear the sweepers as they moved throughout the roads and pathways of the campus where I lived. I remember quiet summer afternoons when these women could be heard slowly, rhythmically coming nearer with enormous grass brooms, sweeping the ground of all the litter and other debris. They neither hurried nor wasted time, but set a pace for themselves and simply persisted. Hot, dirty work, to be sure. But I could tell that the sweepers were engrossed in it, and that being so engaged changed "work" into "sweeping." Sweep by sweep, the sound of sweeping gradually receded into nothingness.

Living in China exposed me to a whole new level of awareness about the kind of resolve human beings can muster to do their work. Once, on an excursion to the sacred mountain Tai Shan, I saw many pilgrims going up and down its slopes by means of a stone staircase—6,000 stairs in all. Even elderly women had climbed to the peak that day and were now coming down the stone steps—*backwards*—loathe to turn their backs on the sacred peak.

By contrast, my family and I stayed on our tour bus, riding half-way up the slope. From there, we waited with other tourists to board a gondola that would carry us to a point near the peak. Freely swinging on its cable, the gondola briskly floated us away into the clouds, while below, the Chinese clung to the stairs. Fifteen minutes later, we were near the top, but still had to climb the ancient stone steps for about twenty minutes in the frosty air. My son was three at the time, and I had to carry him.

Completely exhausted, we finally reached the top and entered what appeared to be a brand new restaurant and bar, opulently appointed with marble floors and gleaming chrome. We ordered beer. It suddenly occurred to me to wonder how all the food and drink for the restaurant had arrived at the top of the mountain—for I knew that the Chinese laborers who served us were not allowed to ride the gondolas. The answer: it had been carried there on foot.

Just outside the restaurant, a man had arrived with a bamboo pole over his shoulders, a case of wine dangling from each end. He had walked up the mountain that day with two cases of wine—no bus, no gondola—just 6,000 stone steps to the top! I asked him how he did it.

"Never stop to rest," he said. "If you do, you'll never get up." He looked to be about 45.

I was nothing like that when I was first getting into Zen. During one retreat, my samu assignment was to sand some oak window sills. At first I had the thought that this wouldn't be so bad; who doesn't like to make wood all smooth? Within a few minutes, however, I discovered that cured oak is granite-hard. It would have taken days for me to complete just one window. No matter how vigorously I sanded away, the 100-year-old stain remained visible. I found this incredibly frustrating, to say nothing of exhausting.

I was attached to an arbitrary distinction between "work" and "play" that meant I couldn't come to the task with any kind of open-mindedness. This attachment was compounded by my belief (again, completely arbitrary) that I needed to hurry, even though I hadn't been given a deadline. This is so typical of the way that "work" must be approached: as a "negative" relative to the "positive" of break time. I had not left myself any room to just sand the windows. And because I couldn't just sand windows,

I couldn't appreciate the wisdom of wood, the wisdom of sandpaper, or the wisdom of my own hands, to say nothing of the wisdom of patience and care.

It took many years of practice before my attachments about "work" were sanded away—and I still have some pretty rough edges! If I had been a little more sensitive to the "choice of place" in which I used my body, the windows would have been sanded in no time. When body, speech, and mind are used carelessly, they are not "placed solid." And that leaves us slipping and sliding on the path of practice.

If, unlike me, you work very hard, you will be able to sand, sweep, paint, and pound nails without using your hands at all. You can even create a piece of land or work the garden soil with a handle-less hoe.

Word Riprap

Which brings us back to the poem. "Riprap" is about making words come to life in the world, exposing reality as it really is. Human beings tend to use words to do this, and working with words can be a lot like working with sandpaper or brooms, carwashes or clothespins. To use words effectively, we have to breathe life into them. In Zen, we make a distinction between the "live" words of genuine insight and the "dead" words of conceptual thinking. Only live words reveal the subtle nature of the Buddha-dharma. Ninety-nine percent of the traditional koan "riprap" that is used in Zen training is the live words of masters and students. The most direct way of learning how to breathe life into those words is to work with a qualified teacher. This kind of word practice not only teaches you how to see things in a most intimate and immediate way, but to express what you see in an intimate and immediate way. This kind of word practice is generally better if you're willing to ask lots of questions. Ordinary questions are fine. When the teacher answers, listen very carefully without thinking about what you're going to say next. That is, listen and try to discern whether the words coming back to you have been "linked hot" to the wisdom of the whole world.

I live in a part of the United States that has a great deal of natural beauty, very near the shore of Lake Michigan. Miles of sandy beaches stretch away to the north and south; looking inland from the smaller dunes near the shore, you can see the enormous dune ridges of the Manistee National Wilderness Area. They are topped by gigantic white pines, and beyond these lie great stands of beech, oak, maple and pine. One time, when my teacher Myoyu Roshi was visiting me, we went for a hike in the forest. It was autumn and leaves covered the ground. After a while, we just walked without talking, listening to the sound of our feet shuffling through the leaves.

"Do you hear that?" I asked.

"Yes, I do," Myoyu Roshi replied. And then she asked me, "Can you hear it louder?"

If you had been there, how would you have answered Myoyu Roshi's question? You know how to make a sound louder, but how would you *hear* it louder? When laid down "before [the] mind like rocks," such words become the "riprap" of the Buddha Way. They will grant you a good secure footing on the long journey home.

The earth-touching gesture by which wisdom and words are "linked hot" can be extremely subtle. This is well demonstrated by a story from *The Book of Equanimity*. In this story, a monk, newly arrived at a temple, is interviewed by the great master Yangshan Hujii (807–883).

"Where are you from?" asked Yangshan.

"I'm from Yu province," replied the monk.

"Do you think of that place?"

"Always," said the monk.

Seemingly banal exchanges like these of the monk and Yangshan can bear motherlodes of spiritual gold if sufficient "torment of fire and weight" is applied. For example, an innocent-looking question like "Where are you from?" might really be asking, "Where are you *at* (spiritually speaking)?" It's like saying, "Touch me with live words, if you can!" The meaning of a deadpan response like, "I'm from Yu province," may likewise not be what it seems.

In this case, both Yangshan and the monk are not engaged in small talk at all. They are discussing the monk's progress at a very sophisticated level. The monk's reply of "Always," is tell-tale. It allows Yangshan to assess the depth and clarity of this monk's insight. A good teacher, he sees that the monk's eye has opened up quite a bit, but it is not open all the way.

So Yangshan said to him, "Thoughts are of the mind. What is thought-of is the world. It includes mountains, rivers, the great earth, pavilions and buildings, people, and animals. Focus instead on the thinking mind. Is there anything there when you do that?" This is like Snyder saying, "What is thought-of is the 'riprap of things.' It includes 'Cobble of milky way, / straying planets, / These poems, people, / lost ponies with / Dragging saddles.' Focus instead on the thinking mind. What do you see then?" How would you answer this particular question? What is the difference between the "thought-of" and your own mind or between "the riprap of things" and your own mind?

As you enter into the realm of live words, you discover just how deeply words affect your understanding of life. Unless you are clear about how language is shaping your world, you may miss the fundamental power of your own mind.

Thinking Mind Riprap

As far as Yangshan's monk is concerned, the wisdom of his attainment tells him that all things are empty, devoid of any inherent self-nature. And because they are, the "riprap of things" are just reflections of his own mind. He sees that his mind and the world are One. His fingers are near enough to the earth that he can feel the electricity of attainment. But he hasn't really completed the circuit. He still has not quite realized that the nature of each rock is a world. So he says, "Doing that [i.e., focusing on the mind], I don't see anything at all."

"That response has reached the stage of faith," said Yangshan, "but it has not yet reached the stage of a human being."

What do you suppose is the difference between the "stage of faith" and "the stage of a human being"? What is the difference between having "faith" and being "human"?

The monk had no idea what to say next, so he just asked Yangshan to help him. But Yangshan would only say, "Take a seat [in the meditation hall] and wear the robe. You must see the next stage on your own."

Do you think Yangshan is being stingy with his Dharma? Why should he bring up important points for his students if all he's going to do is leave them on their own like "lost ponies with / Dragging saddles"?

Intimate with the World

There is more in the foregoing koan than meets the eyes and ears. To take a seat and wear the robe is to get close enough to the earth that you can use it as the robe of liberation. When you are intimate with the world in that sense, you discover that it is not you and other human beings alone who have the gift of body, speech, and mind. "Each rock is a word," means that the Earth speaks just as you do. Getting close to the earth, you can hear and receive that language as it witnesses you in realization. This realization is your meeting the earth on its terms, whether those terms are "straying planets," or "ants," or "lost ponies with / Dragging saddles."

And it is in fact those "lost ponies / Dragging their saddles" that make some of the best riprap of the Buddha Way. Images of large, lost, domesticated animals crop up every once in a while in the wilderness of Snyder's poetry. How did these noble animals get lost? What do you suppose they're about? More importantly, what would you do if you were hiking in the mountains and you came across a horse or a cow that was twenty miles away from the ranch where it belonged? What would you do? How would you feel? What then is "faith" and what then is being "human"?

To fix this problem, you're going to have to get completely involved, completely absorbed in this lost horse, completely committed to covering the twenty miles of rugged terrain that stand between you and the ranch. This isn't a silly problem. This is just how it is when saving sentient beings. They can't do it themselves, and you can't do it for them. The pony can't find its way home, and you certainly can't carry it there. This is what creates the "torment" that fuses the "crystal" of realization to the "sediment" of the world. When "linked hot" in the mind, they become you. When they become you, then all sentient beings are saved.

One of my lost ponies was my son Ben. Born with a mental illness, his illness became the illness of the family—a family with no cure, no change, and no hope. My wife and I, like many parents of children who present unsolvable problems, blamed ourselves. That blame floated through our lives like a thick, dark fog, never settling in any particular place. I think, in some way, we yearned to be discovered in some fundamental mistake of parenting because then we would at least have an explanation for the suffering that we endured when Ben disappeared from school, when he ran away, when he was arrested, when he was brought home in handcuffs, when he abused drugs, when the seizures began. But there was no mistake. Our guilt drifted through our lives, obscuring everything for almost 30 years. There was a horse that was dragging its saddle. Where, we wondered, was the rider? What act of body, what act of speech, what act of mind could bring it the comfort of home?

Then one day there was a change. The change was not in the world of illness, or in the world of pharmaceuticals, or the world of positive thinking. The change came when there was intimacy. I do not mean the kind of intimacy that exists between a parent and a child, though that is certainly included. I mean there was a kind of earth-touching gesture in which illness is illness and grief, grief. It was the kind of intimacy that allowed the great master Yunmen Wenyan (862 or 864–949) to say, that "sickness and medicine cure one another." When you understand how "sickness and medicine" cure each other, your fingers will penetrate the soil of your own life and others' lives simultaneously.

Now I will not be surprised if you have no clue about how to save the pony that is standing on your trail. Even if you manage to save it, there will be another one just as difficult to deal with. This is what touching the earth gets you, what stopping at nothing gets you. You're just stuck. You're stuck building the riprap of your life, just as I am stuck "laying down these words" to give you a foothold on the Buddha Way. As you go along, however, you may discover that you only need very refined grades of riprap, to stay the course of your life. You may even discover that you never needed any riprap at all. And what a wonderful discovery that will be!

To go beyond the riprap of life requires that you become a Buddha. To become a Buddha, you must touch the earth. As soon as you touch the earth, however, the Buddha Way vanishes, and riprap and lost ponies vanish. This is because Buddhas do not need the Buddha Way. More importantly, Buddhas who are no longer on the Way do not remain Buddhas. They do not revert to sentient beings, but they do have a kind of humanity—a manner of being in the world, with conduct marvelous and compassionate beyond compare. If it were not for them, our suffering would be unendurable.

If you really want the whole thing, then relentlessly cultivate body, speech, and mind. Take a seat and wear the robe. The first part is like an arrow that strikes you without feeling. But when the second arrow strikes, it will go all the way to the bone. Wounded, you then must do what you must do, whatever it takes, to save your life and the lives of all sentient beings.

> Fingertips touch the great earth,
> And evening descends over buildings and people.
> At night, in the kitchen,
> She cooks a supper for her family,
> Recalling pleasant days among fields and forests.

∽

Bringing Down the House

Emily Dickinson's Poem "280"

When living on a fluffy, floating world, who thinks about the need for truth?
But when thunder and lightning strike, there is nowhere to go but down.

280

I felt a Funeral, in my Brain,
And Mourners to and fro
Kept treading – treading – till it seemed
That Sense was breaking through –

And when they all were seated,
A Service, like a Drum –
Kept beating – beating – till I thought
My Mind was going numb –

And then I heard them lift a Box
And creak across my Soul
With those same Boots of Lead, again,
Then Space – began to toll,

As all the Heavens were a Bell,
And Being, but an Ear,
And I, and Silence, some strange Race
Wrecked, solitary, here –

And then a Plank in Reason, broke,
And I dropped down, and down –
And hit a World, at every plunge,
And Finished knowing – then –[1]

(1862)

Many readers of "I felt a Funeral" by Emily Dickinson (1830–1886) have tended to think of it as the dark confession of mental breakdown, the morbid self-portrait of the poet as a death-obsessed recluse. Such reactions are understandable. All we know of the "funeral" is that it was a psychological, rather than a physical event. It is a metaphor whose tenor has gone missing, making it all too easy to imagine the worst. To imagine, in other words, that Dickinson's funeral is a symbol of some unnamed, traumatic experience.

I find such interpretations reasonable. And disappointing. They tend to emphasize forms of mental pain and terror (such as nervous breakdown or a nightmarish premonition of death) that actually do not appear in the poem. What *does* appear, from my perspective as a Zen teacher, is a system of images that bear a remarkable similarity to the experience of meditation. There is no reason in the world why we should think that Dickinson would have been unaware of Eastern traditions of introspection; it was part and parcel of the work of many of the Transcendentalist writers whom she admired, such as Henry David Thoreau and Ralph Waldo Emerson. As well, descriptions of the purposes and consequences of Buddhist practice had appeared in a variety of publications that Dickinson might easily have read. But even if she had no formal knowledge of meditative techniques, she nevertheless had the time and space, the quietude and the will of imagination, to turn her light inward and partake of the daily bread of Zen. When considered in that light, "I felt a Funeral" becomes not only a marvelous depiction of the development of meditative concentration, or *samadhi*, but of the collapse of the structures of delusion—what the great master Eihei Dogen (1200–1253) referred to as the dropping away of body and mind.

Take, for example, the parallels between meditation and funeral ceremonies: both are conducted in a planned, rather formal way. Both suggest the need for the absence of distractions that would disrupt the air of solemnity and reflection. And both concern the end of a life—either literally, as in the case of a funeral, or figuratively, as in the case of letting our delusions "die." Interestingly, however, the funeral is interrupted by a pack of restless mourners. They detract from the proceedings in the same way that distracting thoughts undermine the development of samadhi. You may have heard of this is as the phenomenon of "monkey mind": the mind that endlessly chatters, leaps and swings about in your head like a caged animal. It takes some considerable patience to get that monkey to settle down so that you can concentrate.

While monkey mind is a phrase familiar to every meditator, I find the fact that "Mourners to and fro / Kept treading—treading—till it seemed / That Sense was breaking through –," makes a better metaphor for the nature of our usual mental chaos. It registers the endlessly repetitive nature of idle thinking. If you really reflect on the nature of the thoughts that distract you, you'll discover that they are incredibly monotonous. The same miserable thoughts repeat themselves, as Dickinson suggests, "like a Drum" that is "beating–beating." These mourners wander aimlessly around, anxiously unsure of themselves, undecided as to where they ought to sit or what they ought to do. They are a bit of an annoyance, a disruption to what should be a solemn occasion for the "dearly departed."

Getting Seated

Getting the guests of your unruly mind to settle down is like pushing a rope or herding cats. Try as you might, it just doesn't happen right away. Your natural inclination will be to try to *force* your wandering thoughts to be civilized, to demand that they respect your need for peace. But as one of my former teachers explained, "what you resist will persist." If you pick up on their nervousness and fight it, demanding peace and quiet, your "guests" will become even more nervous and agitated. But if you are steadfast in accepting them, your guests will feel that. They will relax and get seated and pretty soon it will all be as though they're hardly there at all.

In other words, if you accept your mind as it is, that changes everything. When concentration begins to form, it does so because you've willed it but also because you've accepted your inability to do it perfectly. It is a somewhat paradoxical moment that is reflected by the delicious ambiguity in the phrase "Sense was breaking through": does that mean that "sense"—the power of discursive thought that is so distracting—is caving in, collapsing? Or does it mean that a new awareness is "breaking through" the crowd of distractions. Either way, a clarifying change is taking place.

Going Numb

The sudden onset of stillness that occurs when your thoughts "all [are] seated" can bring about another, more rarified, form of distraction: fear. Fear of the unearthly quiet. If you're not used to it, it can be quite unnerving. You may feel, as apparently Dickinson did, as though your "Mind were going numb—." This can conjure up frightening notions of brain-death or unconsciousness. In truth, neither of those things can be caused by the practice of meditation. Yet fear of them is common and is one reason why it is especially important, in your first years of practice, to work with a teacher. A teacher can help you contextualize your experiences so that you can avoid such unfounded fears. (Please see my essay "Everybody's Light" for more about this kind of fear.) While I'm certain that most readers of "I felt a Funeral" have not looked positively on the prospect of going mentally "numb," this image seems to me a perfectly reasonable way for a 19th century poet with no formal knowledge of Buddhist meditation to explain the feeling of being released from distraction. It is remarkably similar to T. S. Eliot's description of deep meditative states, which he captured with the word "etherized." From a Buddhist perspective, "mental numbness" means only that the mind does not dally with thoughts. The thoughts themselves may still be there, but their effect on the mind is the same as the effect of physical objects on fingers numbed by cold: no impression is made because the mind is completely unified with the object of meditation (often the breath). "Numbness," as such, is numbness to distracting thoughts and feelings. In their place a relieving sense of clarity and equanimity arises.

Part of getting comfortable with zazen, then, is a matter of learning to enter the stream of awareness, to flow with it, instead of fighting it; to accept it, instead of separating from it. It is a matter of letting go of old, frail attachments. And the more you sit, the clearer it becomes that all the thoughts that have been wearing ruts in your mind need to be allowed to "pass away," to die with dignity. You also learn that there are many such deaths to be encountered in your practice life. If you meditate a lot, you eventually learn that, to fully engage with life, to truly *live*, you must attend a great many "funerals." Given enough experience with these funerals, you will learn how to face your own literal impermanence with greater equanimity.

For her part, Dickinson not only included such spiritually rich "funerals" in the content of her poetry, but reflected the nature of genuine religious undertaking through the *form* of her poetry. I'm thinking specifically of her frequent use of the so-called "hymn meter." Hymns (and much of Dickinson's poetry) follow a four-line pattern that of alternating four- and three-beat lines. Based on English ballads, this meter is sometimes called the "common meter." It is a very regular iambic one—one that would be familiar to nearly every church-goer, making it easier to sing along with the congregation. But the regularity of the rhythm in Dickinson's "hymns" is routinely broken. Nothing, in my view, could have been a greater reflection of Dickinson's distrust of organized Christianity.

Indeed, it was the very organization, habits, and confining attitudes of the Protestant church in America that Dickinson found so antithetical to genuine spiritual work. Genuine spiritual work is messy and hard. It ain't pretty like a stained glass window. The practice of turning your light inward is one in which you must risk cracking open the deeply held convictions and cherished beliefs that religious institutions offer us as reassurance. Dogmas and ideologies of all kinds (including Buddhist ones) are obstacles to spiritual awakening. Because they are conceptual, rather than experiential, they are inevitably limited and wearying, rather than relieving and liberating. It is those "knowns" of religious belief that are often found "treading—treading" through our minds, driving us crazy. To become free, you must let go of the incessant drumming that interferes with genuine, first-hand insight into the nature of your life. You must break away from inherited truths, a point that the poet underscores by breaking away from the metrical pattern in the last line of her poem to "Finish knowing."

As practice deepens, "letting go" is more of a continuous mental activity than it is a sudden breaking away from your conditioning. It is often experienced as a relieving "flow" or "coursing" movement, and it feels effortless. It feels effortless because you are no longer expending unnecessary psychic energy on wrangling bundles of thought-objects into the "person" that you think you are—the anxious "treading, treading" to and fro that establishes the false sense of an enduring self. What you will derive from this is more energy for simply *being*. It is a "thinning of the self" that provides enormous relief.

When the so-called "thinning of the self" begins, you move from what is often called "access concentration" to true *samadhi*—single-pointed, meditative *absorption*. It is here that the spiritual benefits of Zen are realized. Going deeper and deeper into this meditative awareness, you will notice with ever greater clarity and equanimity that, no matter where you search within yourself for the substantive essence of who you are, it cannot be found. That which you may have formerly taken to be a self "dies." The practice of meditation, in this sense, is indeed a funeral that can be "felt" in the brain. Remember, though, that the thing that "dies" was never alive to begin with. It was only an illusion constructed out of the churning of your thoughts. The feeling of "me-ness" is no more substantive, fixed, and enduring than clouds.

In the Empty Sky

But you're probably wondering: if there is no "self" in this "numb" mind, what is it that *hears* "them lift a Box / And creak across your Soul"? These lines aptly reflect one of the most mysterious qualities of deeply absorbed states of concentration: awareness in the absence of thoughts. If you think it odd that Dickinson writes about going numb and yet *hears* "them" in their "Boots of Lead," then you may want to spend some time with a centuries-old koan of the Zen tradition—the question *Who is it that hears?* It is indeed a wonderful to question to ask!

There are other questions that many readers have about this part of Dickinson's poem because there is a confusing sense that the speaker seems to be everywhere at once—perhaps as the deceased in the "Box," perhaps as a witness to her own funeral, and even perhaps as the "soul"-cum-wooden floor over which the pallbearers walk in their "Boots of Lead, again." From the perspective of meditative awareness, this omnipresence isn't confusing at all. In fact, that is exactly how it feels. This level of meditative absorption is one in which equanimity prevails. Without the confining psychology of a fixed "self," you are free to go anywhere in "Space" and experience it in an intimate, immediate way—as your True Self.

This is a crucial point, so I want to emphasize it. When you quiet your mind, when the shambling thoughts have become orderly and still, and you are no longer distracted, it is much, much easier to experience the great release—the miraculous transformation of your mind, from a self-centered matrix of conditioned thinking to the inherently unconfined, unconstrained reality of your true nature. This transformative experience grants access to an infinitely expansive "Space" in which all time vanishes and all things ring with their own self-evident reality "As all the Heavens were a Bell."

I always associate this line ("As all the Heavens were a Bell") to one of the most famous pieces of classical shakuhachi flute music ever composed: "A Bell Ringing in the Empty Sky." It's hard to ignore the similarity. The music was composed by a Japanese Zen monk in honor of Fuke, a legendary Zen master of Tang Dynasty China. Fuke was famed for his wandering throughout the country, ringing a bell. Everywhere he went, he rang this bell. When he died, the villagers put him in a coffin and nailed it shut with his bell in his hand. When they began to bear him away, however, they realized that the coffin was not holding anything. They opened it up and were dumbfounded to discover that Fuke's body was gone! It was then that they heard the distant ringing of Fuke's bell in the empty sky.

You can peel back this metaphor of a bell ringing in the empty sky to discover something of vital importance to your own practice of Zen: *sunyata*, or "emptiness." It's good to be careful not to over-read this word "emptiness." In one sense, emptiness denotes the absence of an unchanging self-essence in phenomena, but that does not mean that things are essentially hollow, or intrinsically "dead." Things are just things. What emptiness actually connotes is a vast, open, unhindered, but palpable space, like the clear, blue sky. The Korean Zen master Seungsahn (1927–2004) has called this the "bone of space." Pretty funny!

Emptiness helps to explain how "Space," which by definition contains nothing, can "begin to toll." Because emptiness is not the same as "nothingness," we cannot say that things don't exist. They do. (If I hit you with my stick, it will hurt because the stick exists and so does your head.) Things nevertheless do not possess a fixed, unchanging nature or "self." To recognize this is to discover that the intrinsic nature of things—including *yourself*—is identical to the *relative* nature of things as they appear in the world. The nature of all phenomenal reality is self-evident. The self-evident nature of Dickinson's "Space," therefore, is what allows it to ring "As all the Heavens were a Bell." This vast, ringing, unhindered space makes it possible for "Being" to be "but an Ear," a deft deglazing of the bell metaphor.

When everything is realized as fully sufficient unto itself, you simultaneously realize that everything is perfect, whole, and complete just the way it is. It can't be any other way. The sense that things are *not* perfect, *not* whole, *not* complete is only possible from the dualistic perspective of self and other, right and wrong, have and have-not—the perspective that is based on the deluded notion that you have a fixed, enduring self. Let go of that faulty notion, however, and then you, I, my dog, the neighbor's car, and the Orion nebula are all perfect, whole, and complete just the way they are. To "finish knowing" things that are not true is to be awakened. But there is more: to be awakened in the absence of a "self" means that all sentient beings throughout space and time must be simultaneously awakened with you.

Everything that you will struggle with in your life and in your practice is a matter of appreciating these awakening relationships—between yourself and other people, yourself and the moon, yourself and the grass. When you realize your nature, then you realize the nature of the moon and grass at the same time. When you realize your nature, the moon and the grass realize you. This is why, when Shakyamuni Buddha attained enlightenment under the Bo tree 2500 years ago, he suddenly declared, "Wonder of wonders! I and all beings and the great earth have simultaneously awakened!"

In Dickinson's poem, the dichotomous (or "dualistic") view that is normally produced by language-thought, and which divides subject and object, self and other, simply ceases to function. If space tolls, being listens. In the depths of concentration, introspection courses along between the poles of effort and acceptance, sustaining one's focus and simultaneously letting go of it. On the one hand, there is the active awareness of a nearly egoless "I," and, on the other hand, the active relinquishing of this "I", which constitutes Dickinson's "Silence."

To construe "I and Silence" as a "Solitary" unity might seem paradoxical. There might be only "Silence" but for the fact that awareness remains. Even this most fundamental and tenacious form of self-clinging, however, must eventually be relinquished. It is the last remnant of what we might call the aware ego, the final "Plank of Reason" to be broken through. To follow the Buddha Way is to allow ourselves to drop "down, and down," hitting "a World, at every plunge." It is to descend through the successive floors of our illusory existence.

It is important to notice the metaphor of collapsing architecture at the heart of Dickinson's poem. It not only describes the descent into successively deeper levels of consciousness, but explains why ordinary thoughts seem so obtuse and lead-booted in comparison to this light, open form of awareness. It also distinctly echoes the collapse of the structures of the false self—a self that was erected, from the Buddhist perspective, by Mara, the demon of delusion. It is quite fitting, therefore, that the Buddha addressed this demon as "the architect." The business of practicing Zen is all about the razing of Mara's architectures of the self.

Normally, however, meditation does not bring the entire edifice down all at once. But there are times when large chunks of it collapse. If our previous meditative training has been sufficient, then these collapses of the house of delusion can be "understood" and cultivated over time to produce much greater depths of clarity. For some people, it happens that the whole house of cards which has been taken to be the "self" collapses and disintegrates. The destruction is so complete that there are not even any "cards" left. This is to have "Finished knowing" or, as is so often said in the Zen tradition, to have "dropped body and mind." It is a shattering renunciation of delusion.

The Ceremony of Fearless Attainment

Keep in mind that Zen is not about going into a trance and staying there. On the contrary, to drop body and mind is an experience that simply allows you to fulfill your daily life. There is often a fear that arises in connection to this; it is hard to let go of the freedom that you feel when meditation is going well. When you stand up from your meditation, it may seem impossible to bring that open, free, expansive sense of things into the ordinary world of working a job, raising children, cleaning the dog poop off your shoe, or washing the dishes. If that happens (and it always does), then you may find it helpful to think about the curative nature of Dickinson's funeral. Now you may wonder how a funeral can cure. But a funeral is a *ceremony*, and the word ceremony is derived from the Latin root *cure*: to *scour* clean; to take *care* of; to *cure*. The "cure," in this case, is to scour yourself clean of your attachments and then to put your "cured" self into the world to cure others—not through any kind of fancy, spiritual hocus pocus, but through spontaneous, un-self-centered appreciation of your life and others' lives. In a way, you could say that the whole point of Zen is to overcome the fears that prevent you from being the generous, ethical, patient, energetic, disciplined, and wise person that you really want to be.

Meditation in that sense is the ever-renewing discovery within yourself of the ceremony of fearlessness. It is to form within yourself the great *mudra*, or hand gesture, of fearlessness that was originally demonstrated by Shakyamuni Buddha. When he lifted his right hand and held it, palm outward, he was making the gesture of fearlessness that reassured his followers. He once stopped a charging elephant by doing this.

That fearlessness can only come from the funeral in the brain that is the death of your self-clinging. It is difficult to attain, but never impossible. If you wish to attain it, just "finish knowing." When you really finish knowing, you will still be able to cook and read and go to work and walk the dog—but you'll do so with greater freedom, joy, and openness than ever before. Funeral by funeral, and day by day, you will discover how to live in relation to all things, serene with cooked peas and cars, diapers and brooms, kittens and the bedroom floor. You will see that all things are perfect, whole, and complete, just the way they are.

Lifting the coffin of Mind,
The floor gives way under the weight.
Above and below, empty sky.
What is the hymn that everyone's singing
To the tolling of a clapperless bell?

1   Dickinson, Emily. *The Complete Poems of Emily Dickinson*. First printing edition. Little, Brown and Company, 1960. Print. 128-129.

Impermanence, Suffering, and No-Self

Tapping the Coffin

Ezra Pound's "In a Station of the Metro"

Ten-thousand flowers return to the one flower. To what does the one flower return?
Saying it, you go blind. Not saying it, you can't see.

In A Station of the Metro

The apparition of these faces in the crowd;
Petals on a wet, black bough.

(1916)

Though it is a very short poem, "In a Station of the Metro" by Ezra Pound (1885–1972) contains within it the vast robe of liberation. It is a completely western poem, yet its mysterious and beguiling lines were written in emulation of Japanese haiku. I am grateful for Pound's determination to communicate the subtle nature of impermanence by way of this centuries-old form of Zen-inspired poetry. Within the poem's dark spaces, I believe you too will find the gift of unborn Buddha-nature. To discover this unborn nature is to live without birth and to die without death. This fundamental fact of being is the formless field of benefaction that we all share.

In outlook, Pound was probably more Confucian than Buddhist, more political than religious, but he was not insensitive to the spiritual dimensions of the human experience. By the time he first published "In a Station of the Metro" in 1913, he had studied and begun to translate Chinese and Japanese poetry for a number of years, alert to the oceanic wisdom to be found there. In combination with the mutual interest of his writer friends and the wave of Orientalism that was then in vogue, Pound realized that the Zen-influenced aesthetics of Japanese poetry, particularly haiku, were the key to revealing the nature of "being in the moment" with greater authenticity, immediacy, and clarity—ambitions that should also be part of our practice as students of Zen.

Perhaps more importantly, Japanese haiku suggested to Pound a structural model for how he and his fellow Imagist poets could focus on the direct and undecorated treatment of a subject without also sterilizing it to death. In this respect, the language of the Imagists has a family resemblance to the "live words" of Zen practice; abstract or conceptual language can simply never reach the intimacy of the Buddha-dharma, the living expression of realization that is all dried shit-sticks and swords, cliff-hanging monks and men stuck in wells. It dallies with donkeys and glittering swords, spreads poison and cuts cats in half. Just so, Pound's poem too is very concrete, relying for its effect on the juxtaposition of two, ostensibly unrelated images. Deprived of explicit correlation, these juxtaposed images are forced to share a dark, ineffable space that that is not so easy to reconcile.

It was exactly this kind of ineffable intensity of perceptions that Pound had experienced one day as he walked through a station of the Paris subway (the "Metro.") "I got out of a train…" he reminisced, "and in the jostle I saw a beautiful face, and then, turning suddenly, another and another, and then a beautiful child's face, and then another beautiful face. All that day I tried to find words for what this made me feel."[1]

Perhaps you too have had such moments—moments when you are moved by a mysterious relationship that appears between the disparate things of your life, but which cannot be directly perceived. Moments that point to a sublime beauty and universality that is palpable, but invisible. If you try to say what it is, you fail—just as Pound did when he drafted a 30-line poem in the hope of capturing his subway experience. A later draft of about fifteen lines was abandoned as well. In the end, Pound realized that the feelings he had had could only be conveyed *indirectly*—something that haiku does exceptionally well. Pruning his poem down to bonsai size, Pound finally had what he called "a hokku-like [haiku-like] statement" that adequately covered the experience.

The first published version of the poem appeared in *Poetry* magazine with a number of blank spaces deliberately inserted between phrases in the lines. These spaces were perhaps Pound's attempt to replicate the sense of sublime, ineffable mystery of his subway experience. Though relatively radical for western poetry of his time, this choice still betrayed a mistrust of the natural, if unspeakable, connection that unites all phenomena. To make matters worse, Pound had inserted a colon at the end of the first line, clearly implying that it was to be read as a mere introduction to the second, more important, line.

These spaces—in both much haiku poetry as well as in the capping poems of the traditional Zen koan literature—reveal one of the most important facets of the direct and immediate experience of living: impermanence. Impermanence is one of the "Three Marks of Existence," along with suffering and the doctrine of the absence of an enduring, changeless self-nature (no-self, or no-soul) that characterize life.

In republishing the poem, however, Pound omitted the unnatural spaces and changed the colon to a semicolon. The change of punctuation was not trivial. By virtue of that little wink of punctuation, Pound (perhaps unwittingly) imported centuries of Zen experience to the tradition of western poetry. And it changed the poem in a most dramatic way: a semicolon suggests that the clauses it joins are of *equal* significance. While a period would not be incorrect, a semicolon suggests that the premise of the first clause *is clarified* by the second, as in the following example:

We did not enjoy the drive home; the roads were covered with black ice.

Pound's semicolon, therefore, implies that "petals" clarifies "faces." But does it? *Exactly how*, you might wonder, *do petals on a branch* clarify the meaning of *faces in a crowd?* In the absence of any explicit explanation, the connection goes unspecified. Empty-handed, you are left with two lines of poetry that sleep side-by-side in the same bed, unaware that they are in a relationship.

To get at the nature of that relationship, a good reader will look for other clues. And a good reader will notice the matter of color. The pale faces in the darkness of the underground correspond to the pale petals stuck to a rain-darkened branch. (Indeed, Pound had said that it was the contrasting colors of the scene in the Metro that had initially triggered his striking emotional experience.) By itself, however, this correspondence of light and dark means nothing—nothing, that is, until you consider another aspect of the traditional haiku that Pound provides to help us: the *kigo*, or seasonal reference.

The kigo is the word "petals"—parts of the blossoms, evidently, of a flowering tree—which tells us that the season is spring. But it is *a particular phase* of spring. It is that brief period of time *after* a tree has blossomed and the flowers have begun to decay. A spring shower has knocked down the loosened petals, and they stick to the wet bark of the tree. The point of this particular kigo is that the flowers, while no longer perfect, whole, and complete, are nevertheless present, luminous, and beautiful—like apparitions, they are the ghosts of "departed" flowers. Together, the kigo and the contrasting light and dark colors seem to allude to matters of life and death, yet the point of the allusion is still not clear. A semantic gap between the two lines remains.

Fortunately, there are other clues to the connection between the two lines. One of these is the amazing unity of sound and meaning, the wonderful mirroring of form and content. Such unity can arise by accident when a poet chooses a word with onomatopoetic qualities, like "apparition." ("Apparition" sounds like what it means; its gentle, lilting airiness mirrors our image of a fleeting ghost.) Pound does much more with onomatopoeia, however. He so meticulously unites sound and meaning, that "In a Station" is almost entirely onomatopoetic. Notice the abundant, softer-sounding consonants of the first line:

The apparition of these faces in the crowd;

These sounds are smooth, hissing, moving, giving the impression of rushing air and rustling coats and umbrellas. Multisyllabic words move faster than do monosyllabic words, so "apparition" rushes by, a fleeting ghost. The crowd flows along to wherever it is going, faces lit like pale lanterns floating in a river of darkness. This beautiful, ephemeral vision is suddenly brought to a full stop, however, by the hard "c" and "d" consonants of the word "crowd," which clearly signal that we have reached the end of the line—in both formal and figurative senses.

As they do, the music of the second line moves at a slower tempo to reflect the relatively slower pace of these strolling passengers. Read aloud, we notice that it is slowed by monosyllabic words and the plosive consonants "p," "b," "t," and "k":

Petals on a wet, black bough.

The "p" sound of "apparition" in the first line is echoed in the second line's "petals," then handed off to its cognate "b" in "black" and "bough." The "t" sound in "petals" and "wet," coupled with the alliterative "p" and "b" sounds in "petals," "black," and "bough," further separate the words of the second line into distinct, discrete moments. In fact, it is impossible to speak the last three words of the poem without a significant silence between them.

This slowed, distinct sequence of individual words mirrors the sequence of individual faces that Pound witnessed in the Metro. (". . .I saw a beautiful face, and then. . . another and another, and then a beautiful child's face, and then another beautiful face.") Then, finally, everything disappears, fading away in the dark vowels of the word "bough."

You may begin to discern from all of this that the "crowd" is a blurry, indistinct, ungraspable "apparition," neither alive nor dead, that floats in a pool of darkness. But once perception is slowed, the most essential constituent parts come into focus, one by one. Like separate petals of a disintegrated flower, the "faces in the crowd" can be seen as a series of separate close-ups, each one revealing a unique set of characteristics that is simultaneously unique and universal.

This way of "seeing" is perhaps the single most important goal of the traditional arts of Japan. Whether it is calligraphy, flower arranging, bonsai, the tea ceremony, or the writing of haiku, the technique of reducing materials to *the fewest necessary elements* is the result of the influence of Zen. It is the sheer brevity of haiku that leads the reader to intently focus on the few sparse words that remain on the page. In *ikebana*, the Japanese art of flower arranging, the artist similarly "edits" or reduces available plant materials to *the least possible amount*, stripping away leaves, stems, and even most flowers, so that the viewer's attention is then fully concentrated on what remains.

But what remains is not just a single flow-er and two leaves. There is also a very con-spicuous, very palpable, empty space between each of the elements of the arrangement: the stems, the leaves, and the foliage. These empty spaces are an equal partner to form. Together, form and emptiness are composed so as to de-scribe a relationship between them that, when fully perceived, induces a stark natural beauty that defies description. The nature of this rela-tionship is wonderfully illustrated by a legend about the medieval Buddhist tea master Sen no Rikyu (1522–1591).

Ikebana arrangement by Yoshiko Nakamura, created for a Cherry Blossom festival. Photo by Joe Mabel.

According to the legend, Rikyu had a garden adjacent to his tea house that was resplendent with morning glories. His garden was so gorgeous that its fame spread far and wide. Even the great Shogun Toyotomi Hideyoshi had heard of its splendor. Wishing to see it for himself, Hideyoshi decreed that he and his court entourage would undertake a trip to Rikyu's home in order to view the flowers.

Word was sent to Rikyu so that he could prepare for the Shogun's arrival. On the day when Hideyoshi arrived, however, not a single morning glory could be seen. Rikyu had cut them all down and pulled up the vines by their roots!

Hideyoshi was known for his terrible temper, so you can imagine how enraged he was at Rikyu's insolence. Such a deliberate thwarting of a shogun's wishes was a capital offence. Upon entering the tiny tea hut, however, Hideyoshi discovered some-thing. There, shining with dew in an understated bamboo container, was a single, exquisite morning glory. Hideyoshi was spell-bound. Comprehending the unspoken meaning behind this single flower, his temper cooled, and he forgave Rikyu.

What powerful meaning had Hideyoshi seen in this single flower that he could not have realized in a garden full of blossoms? The answer to this question lies in the interplay of form and emptiness. By clearing away all the morning glories but one, Rikyu had created a vast empty space within which the Shogun could realize the true nature of that flower—and of his own life. In that sudden moment of intimacy, Hide-yoshi found within himself a garden bursting forth with ten thousand flowers. A tiny tendril reached for the entire universe and took root. There was not another garden like this one in the whole universe. And there never would be again. In that moment, Hideyoshi had seen a million myriad conditions bringing forth life and taking it away.

The Shogun had realized something about the law of impermanence. But what he realized was not merely that life is precious because it is fleeting—he realized that impermanence is the glittering sword of freely giving life and taking it away, a knowledge that goes beyond the mere notion that things don't last. To freely swing the sword of life and death is to understand that impermanence cannot be the real reason for fretting over what we do not have or grieving for what we lose; to swing the sword is to realize that we are free because we cannot lose what we do not have. It was this that caused Hideyoshi to feel—for perhaps the first time in his life—genuine gratitude. He had been freed by a flower.

"In a Station of the Metro" works in precisely the same way. By omitting every scrap of comforting explanation from his poem, Pound created an "empty" space that allows the "faces in the crowd" to be seen as they really are: as forms that arise from, and return to, the darkness, the unborn, the empty space that makes all experience an expression of perfect freedom.

Those of us who live in the west enjoy a tremendous material standard of living, but it is a standard that is based on a faulty assumption: it is the assumption that life's bouquet should never have any open spaces in it. Every space should be filled with flowers. That means we overwork ourselves. Even our "leisure" is compulsively filled up with things to do. It's not just a work ethic, but an aesthetic principle. It will not do that we simply sit in the doctor's waiting room; we must flip through the pages of a magazine. It will not do that students sit still to reflect on what they've learned; they should be studying or at least trying to look as though they are studying. When you were a child, you were no doubt told by your art teachers to "fill up the whole sheet." This is very different from a great deal of East Asian ink paintings that rely on a preponderance of white space in relation to black ink.

The single flower and its two companion leaves in the ikebana arrangement lean into non-existence. The absence of water in a sumi ink painting of a single lotus blooming in a pond tells me that the frosts of autumn will be coming. The "faces in the crowd" are beautiful because there will never be a time when they are not loosening like petals into the darkness of oblivion.

When I respond to the fact of impermanence by stuffing ever more flowers into life's vase, filling up my sheets of paper, my house with bric-a-brac, my stomach with food, I am behaving like a drunkard who has gone in search of another drink. It is to deny the fact of impermanence in my life. And the more that I behave like this, the more meaningless my life becomes.

In the United States, denial of impermanence—and let's face it, it is denial of death—has created a culture of materialism that everyone recognizes is a problem, yet very few of us can think of a remedy. In fact, when the meaninglessness of this material heaven reaches overwhelming proportions, the response is often to go shopping. We are so inured to this pattern of behavior that we do not even notice the subliminal messages that rise up out of the collective unconscious to warn us. Just the other day, I received a flyer in the mail that shouted in big block letters, "Head into summer with no interest!" Below that, in smaller print, it said, "Start shopping today!" Could it be said with any greater clarity? A toxic over-abundance smothers our natural joy of living in the moment.

It is the terror of the cliff's edge, the last-ditch effort to grasp after life. Yet that same precariousness by which the forms of reality leave our hands and our hearts can be the foundation for genuine gratitude. Just as Pound's "petals on a wet, black bough" are all the more beautiful for their imminent passing into non-existence, entering into the space between life and death provides a relief from the desperation that silently chews up our lives.

Case 55 of *The Blue Cliff Record* is an excellent koan that addresses this great matter of life and death. In this koan, Master Daowu Yuanzhi (769–835) and his student Jianyuan go to pay their respects to a family grieving the loss of a loved one. Jianyuan tapped the coffin and asked, "Is this life or is this death?"

Daowu answered, "I can't say."

"Why can't you say?" asked Jianyuan.

Daowu said, "I can't say."

Jianyuan thought about this for a while, but came to no conclusion. As the minutes went by, he became more and more anxious. Finally, on the way home, he said, "Master, please tell me, was it life or was it death? If you don't tell me, I'm going to punch you."

"Punch me if you must," Daowu said, "but I can't say."

Jianyuan did then punch his old teacher. This is a really terrible thing to do. If you ask me, Jianyuan's violence solidified his deluded view of life and death. This delusion lasted so long that Daowu died before Jianyuan realized the truth.

Why do you think Daowu wouldn't say whether it was life or death? Was he just being obstinate? And can you say whether the "apparition" in Pound's poem is life or death, presence or absence?

One morning not long ago, I went into my kitchen to make coffee and saw a single white peony in a vase on the table. I felt a brief pang of sadness, knowing that it would not last. For a moment or two I wondered if the act of picking flowers and putting them on tables were not the most futile act in the world. I stood transfixed, staring at it. The center had a few hidden vermillion streaks among its white petals. The heady fragrance hung motionless in the cool air.

In that moment, I could not imagine the flower any other way than the way it was. The flower had always been and always would be exactly as it should be. It "fit" the world like a lid fits a box. When I looked around the room, everything was like that. Everything was in its place. Everything was exactly where it was supposed to be, doing what it was supposed to do.

What I'm telling you is that while form and emptiness make a great pair of artistic tenets, they are in reality not two things at all. As it says in *The Heart Sutra*, "form is no other than emptiness, emptiness no other than form. Form is exactly emptiness, emptiness exactly form." You might study this statement for a whole lifetime and never exhaust it. It is like trying to strain the light of day out of the darkness of night. "Form is no other than emptiness" is telling you that "faces" are no other than a "crowd," "petals" no other than "a wet, black, bough."

Years after Daowu died, Jianyuan had still not penetrated the meaning of "I can't say life or death." So he went to study with master Shishuang Qingzhu (807–888). One day, Jianyuan walked back and forth in the meditation hall, carrying a garden hoe over his shoulder. He made a great display in front of everyone because his Dharma eye had finally had a glimpse of reality: *form is no other than emptiness*. He wanted to test his spiritual mettle by strutting around, showboating his Zen. When Shishuang asked, "What are you doing?" Jianyuan confidently answered, "I'm searching for the relic bones of my late teacher [Daowu]." Of course those bones had long ago dissolved into the earth. But did Jianyuan care? Form is *emptiness*, he thought. Death is *nothing*. "Petals" are no other than a "wet, black bough."

Jianyuan didn't know it yet, but he was only part way there. He still had a long, long way to go. He had to realize that *emptiness is no other than form too*.

Seeing this need, Shishuang said, "The ocean waves wash the top of the sky. What relic bones are you searching for?"

Jianyuan replied, "That is sufficient for my training."

Do you understand what these men are saying to each other? Realizing that form is emptiness means never having to do a single thing. Of course, you'd be making a big mistake if you thought that "never having to do a single thing" means that you get to lie around like a bag of rice. It doesn't. There are dishes to be done, and the grass needs mowing. To understand Daowu's "I can't say," or to understand the space between darkness and light, you have to see both "form is emptiness" and "emptiness is form." From the perspective of "form is emptiness," the grass gets cut when you stop the mower. That is "never having to do a single thing." "Never having to do a single thing" means that the dishes get washed when you turn off the water. Do you understand?

And from the perspective of "emptiness is form," you mow the lawn without using your legs. Without using your hands, you wash the dishes. If you get this much under your belt, you can dig up the bones of Shakyamuni Buddha with Jianyuan's hoe.

Once you dig them up, however, how will treat them? If everything is empty, you'll probably just toss them in the garbage or run them down the sink or burn them. Is that OK or not? Is respect OK or not? If all you see is that form is emptiness, then respect is for losers. So is love, the law, morality, caring, diligence—the whole shebang. When that's how it is, there is no one to say you shouldn't swagger around the meditation hall with a muddy hoe. When you're on top of the mountain, you feel free from everything—everything, that is, except freedom.

It's incredibly difficult to come down off that mountain. Some people never do. They spend the rest of their lives in a state of smiling, narcissistic misery. They think they are above their feelings of loss, grief, anger, and anguish. The Korean Zen master Seungsahn (1927–2004) used to pose a wonderful koan that fits this situation very well. In it, you see someone walk into the zendo smoking a cigarette. He walks up to the Buddha statue, blows smoke in its face, and knocks the ashes into its lap. It's sacrilege, of course. But this guy is so attached to emptiness that he can't see what he's doing. For him, Buddha is ashes and ashes are Buddha. He has dissolved into the space between the petals of a flower and cannot see the flower. If you tell him that Buddha is Buddha, and ashes are ashes, he'll scoff because words are empty. If you hit him, he'll hit you back (harder) because the precept of non-harming is empty. (Seungsahn explains that this guy is very strong!) How can you get him to see the whole truth, to see that emptiness is form? How can you get him off his mountaintop?

To realize the meaning of this you have to set aside the anguish of mortality and abandon the embrace of freedom. It is to set aside unfounded beliefs in life after death or of a paternal deity that grants life everlasting. It is to embrace yourself as the agent of your own salvation—so there is no birth and death, even as you live and die. It is to say "I can't say," while going to work or washing your hands.

Still, even this is a dualistic view in which we imagine there is *something*. You must go further and see the complete *identity* of form and emptiness. This can only be done with buddha action. It is not enough to accept "faces," "petals," "a wet, black bough," or an "apparition" as empty, transient forms. It is not enough to see that "life" and "death" are both impermanent. You have to be able to say, as master Daowu did, "I can't say life or death" and not be evading the question. Of course, you won't use Daowu's words to say "I can't say." You will have to find your own words to express it. You might not even use words at all. Yet, like Daowu, and like Jianyuan after him, to say "I can't say," moment after moment, is buddha action.

If this is hard to understand, please don't be discouraged. It's really hard for everyone. Master Yuanwu Keqin (1062–1135) said, "If you can't penetrate ["I can't say life or death"], then you must study for yourself and awaken yourself. You mustn't take it easy and let the days go by—you must value the time."[2] Valuing your time means working hard, but it means more than that too. It means to appreciate your life. To appreciate your life means to take responsibility for it. When you're finally really responsible, you come to a kind of serenity and simplicity. Then everything in life is held with two hands as though it were a precious jewel. It is as though your whole life were an altar.

Our altars are wonderful symbolic poems of impermanence. We place a vase of cut flowers on the left. On the right, a candle burns. In the front, a stick of incense smolders, and in the middle a cup of water slowly evaporates. (Or the Buddha drinks it.) Like the faces and the petals of Pound's poem, the objects on our altars are impermanent. Flowers, candlelight, incense, and water cannot last, and these are the things that are symbolically offered to the Buddha statue, the World-Honored One. Do you think these symbolic offerings are appropriate? Jesus got gold when he was born. Why shouldn't Buddha? But in Zen we make beautiful offerings of impermanence to impermanence. Form offers emptiness to emptiness, emptiness offers form to form.

In the language of impermanence, "faces," "petals," "boughs," and "apparitions" are not nouns, but verbs. When you see everything in your life this way, then everything is buddha action. There will no longer be life and death, even as you are born and die. When everything is understood to be exactly as it should be, you will have penetrated "I can't say life or death" and live at peace with yourself.

But if you cannot penetrate "I can't say life or death," then just consider that all the "faces in the crowd" return to the one face that is your own face before your parents were born. This one face will continue endlessly after you pass away. If you understand this, then tell me now, while you're still standing here: to what does this one face return?

> Saving the ten-thousand flowers,
> He does not see the whole ocean
> Washing the top of heaven.
> Using the whole earth as your answer,
> Tell me: Is it life or death?

1   Witemeyer, Hugh. *Poetry of Ezra Pound: Forms and Renewal, 1908-20.* First Edition. Berkeley London, W1Y 1AA: University of California Press, 1969. Print. 34.

2   Cleary, Thomas, J. C. Cleary, and Taizan Maezumi Roshi. *The Blue Cliff Record.* Boston, Mass.: New York: Shambhala, 1992. Print. 321.

An Insufferable Question

W.S. Merwin's "Lake Shore in Half Light"

Geese, descending, trust the autumn water—but what choice do they have?
Gray clouds swirl over the lake, and the boats disappear in the fog.
Along the path, mist does not obscure the old man's shadow.

Lake Shore in Half Light

There is a question I want to ask
and I can't remember it
I keep trying to
I know it is the same question
it has always been
in fact I seem to know
almost everything about it
all that reminds me of it
leading me to the lake shore
at daybreak or twilight
and to whatever is standing
next to the question
as a body stands next to its shadow
but the question is not a shadow
if I knew who discovered
zero I might ask
what there was before

(2009)

Most of us, at one time or another, have noticed a question in the depths of our being—a fundamental question—that has something to do with the meaning of our lives. Taigen Dan Leighton calls it "the question in our nerves that's lit," but, like the speaker of "Lake Shore in Half Light" by W. S. Merwin (1927–), the fundamental question is not an easy thing to put your finger on. The question may be lit and smoldering, but its real power can only be harnessed when we're able to manifest it in our lives.

In Zen, being able to express our understanding is not only an important means by which our teachers verify our insight, but it is itself a manifestation of awakened life. Learning how to speak in the language of the fundamental question that "has always been" requires that we wade out into the deep water of our suffering. It requires that we follow our question to the shore of our lives—and that we then go beyond that shore into a dark, fluid, and dangerous place that we fear.

I live on the shore of Lake Michigan, and I have a healthy fear of its size and power. I have seen its waves swallow whole lighthouses, and I have been caught in rip currents that know no compromise. I have wondered what it would be like to sink far off shore. For summer tourists, the lake may seem like a gentle, perfectly harmless wash of turquoise and bottle-green light, but many sailors and swimmers have drowned in its temper tantrums.

At first, it is pacific, but we come to know that all must flounder in its dark, empty, bottomless water. It is just the same when we wade into the Buddha's First Noble Truth: Life is suffering. When we consider just how enormous that statement is, we may feel that the safety of the shore is far beyond our reach.

In spite of this, however, I know the far shore exists. The knowledge of it is somehow already within me. I may not be able to see or describe or remember it, but "I seem," like the speaker of Merwin's poem, "to know / almost everything about it." It's like having a word right on the tip of my tongue: I feel its presence, and I know it's somewhere within me, even if I "can't remember it."

At times, the fundamental question is so large and mysterious and elusive that it just seems easier to turn my attention to other things. I want to mask its niggling nature in the same way that an oyster protects itself from a grain of sand by covering it with a smooth, round pearl. The sand is not gone, of course, but at least it's out of sight. In the human realm, pearls are made of money, social position, ideologies, and fame. They have a gorgeous luster, but they can never remove what they hide within: a fundamental question that is trying—desperately—to get our attention.

Cutting Up Pearls

If, like Merwin, you are saying to yourself, "There is a question I want to ask," then you're going to have to cut open those lovely pearls and look inside. Of course, destroying pearls is an act society is not usually willing to tolerate. The writer Alan Watts referred to this intolerance as the "taboo against knowing who you are." You could look at it as the taboo against wrecking perfectly good pearls. Why would you do that when you can't be sure what it is you'll find inside? You *might* find something terrible. It probably *is* terrible, or we wouldn't have pearls in the first place. And if you *do* find something terrible, then the truth about life is a *terrible truth*, and everyone is going to have to admit it. They will have to admit that, somewhere deep, down inside of their beautiful pearly world, there is an ugly grain of truth: something is *not quite right*.

When I first started practicing zazen, I was pretty young—a teenager. I hadn't developed any sense for how to talk to others about opening the pearl, about following the lead of the fundamental question. So one day, I told my father, without any particular warning, that I wanted to leave college and go live in a Zen monastery in New York. At that particular moment, we were hurtling down a freeway in bumper-to-bumper traffic at 75 miles per hour. I didn't realize that in naively following the fundamental question to my teen-angst shore, I was throwing an obstacle into my father's familiar path. His foot reflexively shot toward the brake, and for one dizzying moment, I thought we would crash. From his perspective, I had lost my mind.

My father worked a thankless job that paid the bills and kept us fed; my mother did the same. He was dumbfounded by my disregard for all that I had been given. By my ingratitude for pearls. My cheeks burned with shame, and the matter of my living a religious life was never spoken of again for many years.

Some of us, by contrast, are blessed by a strong sense of independence that is capable of standing up to shame and unabashedly placing before us some pretty important, if disturbing, questions. Merwin, for example, has a knack for writing poetry that asks all kinds of uncomfortable questions. He's famed for locating them in the moral universes of war and nature. His questions about violence and human greed, or about whether it is ever acceptable to kill another human being—even if ordered to do so—have earned him the acclaim of many thousands, perhaps millions, of readers who value his poems both as art and as expressions of deep compassion for the suffering of sentient beings. His anti-war poetry of the Vietnam era and, more recently, his environmental writing, all ask important questions that are not easily answered.

Even Merwin's writing style is imbued with a kind of fresh, open wonderment. Absent of punctuation and leaping across unusual line breaks, his poetry's airy, fluttering qualities invite and accept whatever reality blows against its doors. Like an open tent on a summer day, his work flutters and ripples with whatever comes. It is extraordinary in its ordinariness, merging, mixing, and responding to whatever *is*. And, as you will see, it is this open acceptance of what is that both acknowledges the ocean of suffering within us and simultaneously becomes the means by which we reach the far shore of serenity.

A Bowl of Moldy Cherries

To understand how this works requires that we have a more complete view of the nature of suffering. So let's take a moment to be very clear about it. It's not that life has suffering *in* it, as though life were a bowl of cherries with a few moldy ones tossed in just to make us miserable. It is that life *is* suffering. It isn't anything else. *All* the cherries are moldy. Now you may think that sounds pessimistic, but, as I said above, it is actually the all-pervading nature of suffering that is the avenue to our release from it. How is that possible? How is it possible that such an ocean of suffering could be the self-same field of liberation promised by the Buddha? If suffering is as vast as it seems to be, how can there be any hope of living a life of happiness and joy?

The honest answer is that there can be no hope. I'm not saying that because suffering is universal we never have moments of joy, happiness, contentment, or peace. Those things happen; they're very pleasant. What I am saying is that no matter what we feel—whether it is pleasant, unpleasant, or just neutral—our lives never exist outside the realm of suffering because they never remain any *thing* at all. Suffering is universal because impermanence is universal. Impermanence means that all things change. Sooner or later, therefore, as all things come into, and go out of, existence, we lose the pleasant things we have, and the pleasant things we yearn for do not come to pass. The thousands that we invested in stocks and bonds will be lost, and the fame we so richly deserve will never materialize. Impermanence means too that the unpleasant things we would like to dump cannot be dumped. It means that the things we wish to avoid will nevertheless be plopped right at our feet. To *hope* is therefore to wish for a reality that is anything but real.

We can also say that hope is the desperate belief that our view of how things should be can perpetually overcome our experience of how things are. We are so conditioned to think this way that almost everything in our lives is subject to this faulty sense of hope. Just now, for example, my refrigerator made a strange noise. (The manual said this would happen.) Even though I've had this refrigerator for several years, it still manages, from time to time, to surprise me with a new, strange noise. When I hear it, I stop what I'm doing, lift my head, and listen, trying to hear the sound again. I fret that something is wrong. I wonder whether I can afford to have the machine fixed. I blame the manufacturer, and desperately fantasize suing the company. Why do I do this? Because instead of trusting my *experience* (that I heard what I heard), I trust my *view*—which is that my refrigerator shouldn't make that kind of noise. My refrigerator is a machine. It should be perfect, consistent, unchanging. When I can't simply hear the sound once and accept the simple fact that I heard it, I suffer.

Even when we think we're willing to acknowledge the truth, our long conditioning of denial can cause us to postpone an honest reckoning with our intellectual oyster shells. Once, when I was out shopping, I picked up a large box and noticed that my hands had slipped on a white powder. I didn't think much of it but wiped my hands on my coat and walked toward the cashier with my box. Before I had even finished paying, however, I was beginning to wheeze. (I have asthma.)

On the drive home, my hands itched so much that I had to scratch with one hand, while I steered the car with the other. My neck and my face broke out in hives. I drove home and puffed on my emergency inhaler. I had the annoying thought that I might be in need of serious medical attention. But instead of going to the emergency room, I drove to the pharmacy and bought an analgesic ointment.

I smeared it in a thick layer all over my body and waited for relief. None came.

I knew that the itching was not merely on my skin, but inside of me. (Take heed!) But I stubbornly clung to seeking relief in the wrong place, prolonging my misery. The thought that I should be going to the hospital plagued me, but I didn't go. It just irritated me to think of having to do that. *Besides*, I told myself, *the itching is surely just about to stop.*

I can deal with it, I thought.

But the itching continued.

It was not until I was convinced—several writhing, miserable hours later—that I couldn't save myself on my own, that I began to consider going to the emergency room. I had postponed the obvious solution as long as possible, out of a hope that my *view* would trump *experience*.

I feared that the hospital staff might be unable to help me, (so it all would have been a waste of time).

I feared that the hospital staff would ask me why I hadn't come in sooner (which would make me feel stupid).

I feared that the hospital staff would laugh at the guy with the itch (which would make my misery seem trivial when what I wanted was to be taken seriously).

But I had tried everything I knew, and everything I knew had failed to work. So, feeling a little stupid, a little embarrassed, and pretty helpless, I went to the ER. The staff shot me full of epinephrine and wrote a prescription for steroids. I left in a state of humbled relief. I never found out what that white powder was, but I had learned something far more valuable about myself: that I will go to extraordinary lengths to secure the illusion of control and certainty, compounding my suffering and the suffering of others. I learned that it often takes a dramatic event in one's life to realize that suffering really does exist and that it is in the very nature of life. In other words, I learned just how much more I valued my *view* of what should be than my *experience* of what is.

This is why I often say that Zen is the path of last resort. We come last to what should have come first. Even if we think we came to Zen early or easily, a careful examination of our motives inevitably reveals a failure of some kind to scratch that fundamental itch with money, fancy food, material wealth, fame, or by simply pretending to be satisfied with the status quo. It is only *a systemic failure* that clears the decks of all pretenses to perfection or righteousness that opens the way to the reality of suffering: you can't hope your way out of it. Life is suffering, a whole lake full of it. Like Lake Michigan, it is so wide, you can never hope to see the other side of it.

Submission

If life is suffering, and insurmountably so, how then can we escape it? The answer to that is in the tiny, little poem at the head of this essay. Don't be fooled by Merwin's informal tone; he's driving at one of the most important features of our practice. It is the one single thing—the one simple, moral, immediate, personal, and *natural* thing—that can end your suffering right now: to get acquainted with the fundamental question.

The fundamental question, however, is not like other questions. It cannot be asked (let alone answered) in the same way that you ask ordinary questions. What you have to do instead is to submit yourself to it. This is important, so try to absorb it: the fundamental question *cannot be asked*. What it needs is your willingness to submit to it.

Most of us find the notion of submitting to anything an unappetizing proposition. Americans, being reared in the lap of individuality, are usually quite suspicious of the whole idea of "submission." It connotes a demeaning of the self, a willing self-victimization.

Yet nothing could be further from the truth. True submission is none other than an acceptance of how things are. It is an acceptance of the *real*. To put it in terms more appetizing to Americans, submission is acceptance of one's *experience*. Whenever we sit *zazen* (seated meditation), we submit ourselves to experience. We sit with the fundamental question. In zazen, the fundamental question leads, and we follow. Please be clear! You are not the servant of another! To "follow" the fundamental question in this context is to awaken to your own experience, to what you already know. It is a process by which you align your experience with a *view* that for once makes sense. That view—what the Buddha called "Right View"—is that life is suffering.

It sounds easy enough, but it is actually quite hard to do. You start out feeling that you "can't remember" what the fundamental question is all about, so you let it lead you "to the lake shore / at daybreak or twilight / and to whatever is standing / next to the question / as a body stands next to its shadow." But why does this question lead you to a lake shore? Why doesn't it lead to the living room or the airport? Why doesn't it lead to India or Japan or the pool hall down the street?

If you wade into these words very slowly, very carefully, they start to come clear. It is day break or twilight, when the opposing qualities of day and night merge and become one. (See my essay "Course Correction" for some details about "twilight speech.") Because I live by one of the Great Lakes, I know too that those are the times when the water and sky are the same color. The horizon disappears and water and sky—seemingly the whole world—merge and become one.

But this doesn't happen only in the natural world. It happens on another level whenever we sit zazen. In zazen, we open ourselves "…to whatever is standing / next to the question." Whatever comes *is* our view at that particular moment. Experience and view merge and become one. In the Zen tradition, this "oneness" is often metaphorically referred to as "the true body." Thus, Merwin is creating a syllogism: the question is to the lake shore as a shadow is to the true body. The fundamental question, then, leads to the liminal place of inherent division, a place where land and water meet. But this meeting of land and water is as a shadow cast by the true body of oneness.

When I consider this, I realize that Merwin is not necessarily writing about an actual lake, but about the experience of zazen which he practices for 45 minutes each morning and evening. The fundamental question, therefore, is that urge within us to bring about an alignment of our view (that land is land and water is water) and our experience (that land, sky, bodies and shadows, questions and answers, constitute a single ocean of reality).

But there's a hitch. The "…question," Merwin tell us, "is not a shadow." If the question is not a shadow, then, by implication, the body is not a body. What does this mean?

The Ocean of Suffering is Stone

Zen practice is a tricky business because every insight you have is an insight that will eventually crumble away—including that all things are One. It may be helpful at some point in your practice to realize that the world is not just a dualistic matter of pearls and not-pearls, or to realize that all things are the pure, vast reality of the true body. But if you stop there, contented with this little insight, all you have done is to adopt another pearl. It might be shinier and brighter than other pearls, but it's a pearl nonetheless.

Insight after insight, you go on practicing. You have to continue seeing into the nature of reality a little more each day. Gradually, the gap between self and other, sand and pearl, and faith and doubt, is closed. Sometimes it seems you are so close to closing that gap that there is nothing left in the whole world, nothing left over, no misalignment of view and experience, no pearl, sand, self, other, sickness, old age, or death. Just nothing. Zero. But the truth is that you never quite get there. You never perfectly close the gap once and for all. And that means that you always will suffer a little bit. It means that the extent of suffering is infinite.

Fortunately, the extent of wisdom and compassion are also infinite. But how can both things be true? In the Zen tradition, we have a koan that speaks to the challenge of reconciling infinite suffering and infinite emancipation from suffering. If you can crack this koan, it will be easier to understand how it is that suffering can be the field of liberation. The koan is *How do you get out of a stone grave that is locked from the outside?* This koan is actually another way of asking how it is you can bring your experience and your view into alignment. You could also say that it is all about finding the end of suffering in suffering itself.

To work with this koan, you first have to put yourself in a very frightening, uncomfortable place—one in which your whole being must be brought to bear on that heartless stone. Whatever you do, it's going to take an extraordinary act to get out of the crypt. There is no door, no window, not even a crack. The stone is two feet thick, and it goes deep under the ground. They say Bodhidharma, the First Zen ancestor teacher, got out of such a crypt, and they say that Jesus did too. How are you going to do it?

If you don't want to die of suffocation or thirst, if you don't want to die all alone in the cold, dark tomb, you will have to really raise the fundamental question of life and death. Only when you raise this question will you be able to pass your whole body and mind right through stone. You might think you can become like one of those mothers you sometimes hear about—she lifts a car with her bare hands to free her trapped child. You might think you can just punch your way through solid rock. If that's what you think, I wish you the best of luck. If you cling to your view at the expense of your experience of the hard stone of suffering, then you're going to end up with some mighty sore knuckles.

In other words, *if you doubt your experience, you'll die of your view.* That's all there is to it. Your last few minutes on Earth will be spent in the futile attempt to break solid rock with your bare hands, or quietly whining to yourself about the unfairness of your life. You will struggle against that implacable stone, or you will struggle against the people who you think have put you in the ground. As long as you stick with the game plan of hiding, denying, or postponing the acceptance of your situation, you'll never get out of that terrible place.

My own experience with this koan was one of the most anguishing things I've ever gone through. It took me months to come to grips with it, months of hurling myself against the stone of my own stubbornness. Partly, this was the result of male conditioning to have that ready "answer" for every potential problem. It was also just my arrogance. *I can take care of myself,* I thought. Eventually, however, a catastrophe ensued: I failed—it was *a total systems failure*—to get out of the stone grave. In just that moment, almost as if by magic, the tomb in which I was trapped suddenly dissolved, and all space and time opened up like a vast and endless lake. I was free.

Out in the Middle of the Lake

Now you may think that this koan is all about letting go, all about giving up a view of escape that could never work—that perhaps this koan has something to do with accepting one's "fate." After all, isn't that why we practice Zen? Isn't it to learn how to accept our lives just as they are? Of course it is. But how do you think a mother seeing her child pinned beneath a car would go about accepting her situation? Do you think she would just shrug, and walk away?

When you can't break out of the tomb, and you can't convince yourself that it's just a dream—and when you can't wait for a better time to figure things out—then the only thing you can do is to realize the nature of the tomb. This is just another way of saying that you must ask the fundamental question. The tomb is "standing next to the question as a body stands next to its shadow," except that the question is not a shadow and the tomb is not a body. To ask the fundamental question is to submit yourself to this perfect mystery. This submission is a miracle of resurrection known to the likes of Bodhidharma and Jesus. You can know it too.

When you realize the fundamental question, all of your suffering is right here, right now. When your suffering and the suffering of all beings is right here, now, it is not different from you. That's why you can't "remember it" or see it directly. It's impossible to say exactly what it is because it's inconceivable. It could almost be nothing, it could almost be "zero." But to say it is "nothing" or "zero" is to posit that there *is* something. This is why Merwin ends his poem with the statement "if I knew who discovered / zero I might ask / what there was before." What do you think was there before? How do you peel away the layers of nothing at all?

To resolve the matter fully, you must allow your suffering to fill you up. Just see your life as nothing but desire, nothing but utter *want*. Nothing but *suffering*. Don't imagine that you have any place to which you can escape. You don't. Life is suffering. When every molecule of your life, everything you have done and will do, is the manifestation of this illimitable reality, you advance beyond purity, beyond Buddha. Then suffering ends.

The tomb opens.

You are reborn.

All I'm telling you is that you must have a great realization of suffering. Then it's easy to see why it is the one, fundamental question we all share. Raise and cherish this fundamental question. Enter the ocean of dazzling light. Meet the unmet person face to face, this Buddha going beyond Buddha.

Who dares ask a question?
Who dares challenge what cannot be challenged?
All I know is this:
It's better to have the one pearl
If one pearl is all you have.

Everybody's Light

T. S. Eliot's *East Coker*

The darkness of the coffin's interior is exposed to the light! If you're afraid, just remember:
Old Possum is playing dead again. Your job? Take his place in the smokeless crematorium!

from East Coker

O dark dark dark. They all go into the dark,
The vacant interstellar spaces, the vacant into the vacant,
. . . .
And we all go with them, into the silent funeral,
Nobody's funeral, for there is no one to bury.
I said to my soul, be still, and let the dark come upon you
Which shall be the darkness of God. As, in a theatre,
The lights are extinguished, for the scene to be changed
With a hollow rumble of wings, with a movement of darkness on darkness,
And we know that the hills and the trees, the distant panorama
And the bold imposing façade are all being rolled away—
Or as, when an underground train, in the tube, stops too long between stations
And the conversation rises and slowly fades into silence
And you see behind every face the mental emptiness deepen
Leaving only the growing terror of nothing to think about;
Or when, under ether, the mind is conscious but conscious of nothing—
I said to my soul, be still, and wait without hope
For hope would be hope for the wrong thing; wait without love
For love would be love of the wrong thing; there is yet faith
But the faith and the love and the hope are all in the waiting.
Wait without thought, for you are not ready for thought:
So the darkness shall be the light, and the stillness the dancing.

(1940)

"Earthrise."
Photo by Apollo 8 crewmember Bill Anders.

On Christmas Eve, 1968, the astronauts of Apollo 8 took a photograph of the Earth as it rose over a gray crust of the moon's horizon. Known now as "Earthrise," the photo has since become one of the most frequently seen images in the world. When I look at this image, I am captivated by the beauty of that lonely blue jewel in space. It seems so serene and peaceful that it is hard to imagine that it is the locus of so much greed, anger, and ignorance.

Around the sun go oil spills, drug cartels, terrorism, climate change, torture, racism, and rape. Blood drips through the darkness. The litany of humanity's cruelty stands in stark and ironic contrast to that blue, serenely dwelling jewel.

So what shall we do? Our daily dance on planet Earth can seem a downright discouraging mess. Many—most, actually—of my college students won't read the news because it is just too discouraging. From their point of view, the world is, as T. S. Eliot (1888–1965) writes in this excerpt from *East Coker*, "dark dark dark." But the world is not just dark externally; the same darkness resides within as well. To face that external darkness without fear requires that you "go into the dark" that lies within. That interior darkness is the mark of existence known as *anatman*, or "no-self." Anatman refers to the absence of a fixed and enduring self-essence or soul. For many people, that idea is the hardest aspect of Buddhist practice to accept. It provokes a terror as of imminent death or non-existence. But if you carefully investigate Eliot's poem, and learn how to conceive of this particular form of darkness, then the lack of a self is no longer a terrifying, "vacant" space, but the opening of the field of liberation. Indeed, as the poet writes, "the darkness shall be the light."

Before that light can be seen, however, the darkness must be engaged. To do that, Eliot suggests, you should "Be still, and let the dark come upon you."

To "be still" in the face of the darkness is to focus your mind in the practice of *zazen*. In zazen, the stillness of non-attachment allows you to investigate the mysterious, dark, underlying nature of reality without concern. "The stillness" of your mind is what allows "the dancing" of your awareness. And when your mind is well-focused, you are aware of nothing in particular. It is called "darkness," but it is not darkness in the scientific sense of the absence of light. It is just a matter of going "into the dark" of not-knowing.

To understand how the darkness can be the light, you have to carefully consider Eliot's characterization of the darkness. He does not spare you your feelings about yourself, but marshals three distinct similes to help you understand that the darkness he is speaking of is only superficially terrifying.

The first simile explains that the darkness is like that "in a theatre" when "the lights are extinguished, for the scene to be changed." I deeply appreciate this particular simile. It deftly conveys the idea that it is darkness, not light, that is the fundamental state of things, (which, in a theater, is *added* to the environment). The simile also suggests that the world we've been living in is nothing more than a stage set, a cardboard version of reality that we usually think of as the *only* reality. When that vision of "hills and the trees, the distant panorama / And the bold imposing façade are all...rolled away," we are left in a "darkness on darkness."

Eliot's second simile explains that the darkness is as "when an underground train, in the tube, stops too long between stations," and the passengers are left with a "growing terror of nothing to think about." This comparison helps us understand the darkness from a more personal point of view—from the perspective of one who encounters the darkness without the proper context. When that happens, the absence of light (which is a metaphor for the absence of thought) is experienced as a frightening mental blankness.

Finally, Eliot's third simile compares the darkness to the effect of ether (an obsolete form of anesthesia) in which "the mind is conscious but conscious of nothing—." (It should be said that meditation is not really like being anesthetized, hypnotized, entranced, "zoned-out," "spaced-out," or other similarly inaccurate comparisons.) Like the subway simile, Eliot's comparison is a bit idiosyncratic, but it conveys no sense of terror. The mind looks neutrally upon the darkness without the distraction of emotion or judgment. Here, Eliot is relying not so much on any understanding of medicine as on his understanding of Buddhist consciousness.

This darkness, then, is one in which a false world is "rolled away," leaving the terror of a cognitive blankness—and it clears the mind of everything but consciousness. While this prospect may not at first appear attractive, I have to ask you: what could be more valuable than the quiet suggestion to be patient while looking into (what the Zen tradition calls) the "great matter of life and death"? And what, after looking deeply into the unknown darkness, could be more valuable than overcoming your fear of it? What, to come at it from another perspective, is more valuable than knowing the truth, even if the truth means the death of an idea?

Entering the Silent Funeral

Eliot anticipated his readers' fear of darkness quite well. He himself was well acquainted with the terrifying kind of darkness that keeps people huddled in small pools of light, afraid for themselves. When Vivienne, Eliot's first wife, began to show signs of mental illness, he plunged into a deep despair. Unwilling or unable to care for her, he began to avoid her altogether. It was during this difficult time that Eliot seriously considered conversion to Buddhism.[1] By 1938, Vivienne was committed to an asylum, and a year after that, as England was falling into the inferno of World War II, Eliot began to compose *East Coker*. The poem urged its readers—as had all the Indian mystic poets and philosophers that Eliot had studied at Harvard—to go "into the silent funeral" at the center of "the darkness of God." You too can overcome your fears and look deeply and dispassionately at the truth of your life—a truth that has the power of life and death, though it grants no more life than already exists here and now, and brings death to no more than a cherished notion of the self.

All of this may be hard to accept because the "self" that enters "nobody's funeral" feels as though it is alive. Of course, it's not alive, but most of us nevertheless treat our notions of "selfhood" as though they were living things in need of our help. For hundreds of years, students of the Zen tradition have considered this human proclivity to be something on the order of dragging around a corpse and worrying about its welfare. To force the issue into the open, therefore, students may meditate on a koan that aims to undermine this fundamental delusion: *Who is dragging this corpse around?* It is a powerful reminder that nothing about one's self is substantive, nothing about it is sacred, nothing about it is beyond the reach of change and impermanence. Search through your life as you will, search as long as you like, but you will not find a fixed and enduring self within you.

To "go into the silent funeral" means to turn light and darkness on their heads. You can do this through the diligent practice of zazen, or meditation. When you are calm and equanimous, you can see that the "darkness" you fear is all about your fear of death. This fear has motivated you to keep the lights constantly shining on a fantasy stage set, helping you ignore a fundamental truth about yourself. That kind of light is a blinding darkness. When you let it go out, you discover that the real darkness you feared is really the "darkness of God," a pure light within which the illusory "self" no longer appears. In fact, it was never real.

The medieval master Gaofeng said that the koan *Who is dragging this corpse around?* frightened him "out of his senses." It forced him to reckon with himself in a way he never had before. And what he began to discover was that he had been living a lie. Everything that he had ever done in his life had been for the sake of a "self" that he could not find. It was most disturbing! To realize that you are living a lie is to realize that you are, in fact, a corpse—a living, breathing, walking, talking corpse.

After meditating for a week on nothing but this koan, Gaofeng "smashed" through it into a great enlightenment experience. He was, in his words, "restored to life."[2] How do you suppose Gaofeng's corpse became the basis for the restoration of his life? If you think there are living bodies and lifeless corpses, then you'll miss it.

Staring into the Gap

I remember my first encounter with the realm of darkness. It happened on top of the high bluffs that overlook the Portneuf Gap in southern Idaho. I had hiked one cold evening to the top of the bluffs so that I could be alone and ruminate on the dreary fact that I had lost a job—not because I was incompetent, but because I simply wasn't needed. And now, with little in the bank, I had only a handful of days before the food ran out, and I didn't know what I was going to do then.

Below me, the silent lights of Pocatello gleamed through a cloud of woodsmoke like stars nestled in astral haze. I knew people down there were talking, driving, watching TV, and putting their kids to bed. There was a world of needs and wants—and probably satisfactions too—all wound into the cloth of a moonless night.

I stared, transfixed. There was not a sound to be heard. All alone, I lit a cigarette and felt a kind of gentleness overtake my body. Suddenly each of the tiny lights in the valley were just one light, and the one light appeared as a kind of darkness. This darkness—the darkness that was all around, and through me, and through all things—was the only thing.

I felt as though my breath were entwined with all the dreaming world, with all the late-night drivers, and lovers, and sleepers. With the chilled and aromatic sagebrush, the subtle glints of snowflakes teetering on the tips of dried grasses. There was a distinct clarity that the burden of being "me" had somehow slipped away. What are troubles to the reaches of inner darkness but more darkness? To the sweet and simple darkness that is not the same as, nor different from, the darkness of night? The darkness of night had only encouraged a stilling of my mind, and, stilled, I went into the darkness within.

The experience did not last long. I came back down the slope, into the noise of streets and cats and midnight dogs—the warmth of my own kitchen. I had gone up to the top of the bluffs with the "I" that suffers, and I came down with the robe of darkness draped gently over my shoulders. I still had my problems; I was out of a job and out of money, but I wasn't afraid anymore.

The robe of darkness is a shared robe. It is passed on throughout all space and time, worn by each and every one of us, whether we realize it or not. It is truly the formless field of benefaction that comforts our troubled, spinning world.

To see how the robe of darkness fits you, you must work hard at your own practice of zazen, work hard at your practice of being still, just as Gaofeng did. When you too smash through the darkness, it becomes something else: it becomes light. Life becomes death. And death, no longer as you once knew it, becomes your true life.

This is why the Zen tradition not only uses corpses as the basis for koans, but as a form of praise, a way of saying you have let go of something that wasn't real. Take, for example, the story of a monk who asked master Shishuang Xingkong (n.d.) to tell him the ultimate meaning of Zen.

"If you can tell me how to get a man out of a well without using a rope," said Shishuang, "then I'll tell you the meaning of Zen."

The monk responded, "I hear that master Chan of Hunan province has wonderful things to say to the people there."

Upon hearing these words, Shishuang called out to his attendant, "Hey, come in here and drag this corpse away!"

In this case, the corpse was the enlightened body of a monk, a person who had completely let go of his stage-set self. To be called a corpse was high praise. Indeed, the "great death" is a long-standing Zen trope for a very deep and clear enlightenment experience.

Show Me Your Light

So let me ask you: Who *are* you? Don't say "John," or "Jennifer," "A teacher," or "A plumber." Don't say "My-name-is-Leslie-and-I'm-a-32-year-old-wife-and-mother-living-in-Cleveland,-Ohio." None of that is the essential "you" that is under the hood. All of that stuff could change. Who is the "you" that is the changeless you? Who are you when the theater goes dark or when the train stops between stations and there is nothing to talk about? How would you answer the question if you were "etherized?"

If you take this question as it's intended, and if you don't try to evade it or come up with clever "Zen" answers, you may find it very difficult to answer. Maybe it would be easier for you if I were to ask, *What is your light?* Forget about darkness and funerals and death and corpses. Just show me your light!

This was the approach that the great master Yunmen Wenyan (862 or 864–949) took in Case 86 of *The Blue Cliff Record*.

"Everyone has a light," said Yunmen to his monks. "When you look for it, you don't see it, and all is dark. What is everyone's light?"

The monks couldn't come up with an answer to Yunmen's question, so he had to answer for them. He said, "The kitchen pantry and the main gate."

Can you see what master Yunmen is doing to help his monks understand? It's really the same thing that Eliot is doing in his poem—trying to get his monks to face facts. He's trying to get them to search everywhere—under every rock, behind every wall, beyond even the sky and the interstellar spaces—for the self that each one of them believed exists.

"The kitchen pantry and the main gate." It's so unbelievably clear! It's the briefcase in my chair. It's the robin chanting outside my window. But if you think you can just come up with some goofy non sequitur to answer the question about your light, think again. It's not that easy. When master Yunmen heard the deafening silence after his "kitchen pantry and main gate," he added a little something else to complete the picture. He said, "A good thing is not as good as nothing at all."

How can he say that? How can he say that nothing is better than a good thing? Did his mother teach him that?

When you peer down inside Yunmen's words, you just might see what's going on. What is a "good thing"? What is "nothing at all"? If you're thinking that Eliot's "darkness" or his "vacant going into the vacant," is somehow connected to Yunmen's "nothing at all," you're on the right track. You should think about this too: is the kitchen pantry or the main gate "a good thing"? Or is it too just "nothing at all"?

To get to the bottom of your life and dredge up the ultimate nature of your being means sitting in the faith that it is alright for things to be whatever what they are. If you're like most people, however, you may lack the kind of faith that is necessary to do that. Unfortunately, most of us substitute hope for genuine faith. We hope— through the activity of our ceaselessly churning, ruminating, rationalizing thoughts— that the light focused on the stage of our lives will stay lit. It is a desperate wish to stay in control of what cannot be controlled. As long as you struggle to keep the stage lights on, you cannot see the darkness for what it really is: Light. The *real* Light.

So I'll make you a deal. If you can show me a self that is fixed, enduring, change-less, and particular to you, then by all means keep your hope. But if you *can't* show me this self, then give up your hope that you can keep it alive forever. Hope is not your friend. Faith is your friend. This is why Eliot writes, "be still, wait without hope / For hope would be hope for the wrong thing." And it is the same for love. He writes: "love would be love of the wrong thing." It is really such a remarkable insight! If you think about the experience of love, it is all about your feelings of affection for others. But those others—who are they? What *is* it that you love if neither you nor they have a "self"?

It is even the same for thoughts. Those thoughts! Those thoughts! How they grow like weeds in the mind! You think you've pulled them up by the roots, but there they are again! And it is thoughts, more than anything else in life, that make it seem like there is a "me" somewhere down inside your big-messy-wonderful-chaotic-joyous-and-sometimes-frightened-but-ever-changing life. But is it there? Look hard! Eliot writes, "Wait without thought, for you are not ready for thought." Penetrate into this most important question! Look into it with passionate courage. Look into it like there is no tomorrow—because there may not be one!

That is exactly what Case 28 of *The Gateless Gate* is all about. In this case, Deshan Xuanjian (782–865) was brought to a dramatic turning point in his life when he real-ized the limitations of his intellectual views. (For more on the significance of spiritual turning points, see the first essay in this book, "Course Correction.") At the time he came to this turning point, Deshan was a scholar of Buddhism well-known for his understanding of *The Diamond Sutra*. Seeking to test his understanding against the spiritual prowess of an esteemed master, he paid a visit to Longtan Chongxin (n.d.). The two men talked and talked, long into the night. When it was finally time for Deshan to depart, he opened the door and saw that it was pitch dark outside.

"It's so dark!" he said to Longtan.

Longtan went back inside, lit a candle, and offered it to Deshan. Just as Deshan reached out for it, however, Longtan blew it out. Deshan was suddenly enlightened.

The next morning, Deshan went out with his large collections of scholarly commentaries on *The Diamond Sutra* and burned them. He had seen the vast oceans of brilliant darkness that lie beyond mere thinking.

Darkness Following Darkness Is Light

We are so lucky that there is always a way for us to do this important work of looking in. That is the practice of zazen. When you sit in zazen, your stillness is ideally not a quietude that is "like" or "unlike" something else. It is incomparable. In zazen, there is nothing to know and no one to know it. It is like a continuous running of a stream through the darkness. In zazen, you "wait without hope, without love, and without thought"—not because you despair, or feel alone, or are confused. The emphasis is not hope, love, or thought, but on waiting.

In a sense, you can think of zazen as a matter of waiting. If you are actually waiting and not doing something else too, then you are not impatient to be on your way. You are not worried about when the lights will come on again. You just wait. This waiting is not passive. This waiting is the unity of your faith and your love. It is not faith *in* something; nor is it love *of* something. This faith and love, Eliot tell us, "are in the waiting" itself. This is because in zazen you can find a deep resonant contentment with the ways things are, just as they are, and when you do, then all—and I do mean *all* things—are waiting with you.

To wait like that—or let's say, to *abide* in the absolute nature of no-self—is to come upon the most beautiful understanding of all. It is the understanding that "we *all* go" into the dark. It is not the case that just *some* of us go. It is not the case that some stay behind, terrified that their theaters will go dark, that their trains will stop between stations, or that they will end up etherized upon a table. There may be people who are afraid, but the darkness that they experience *also* goes "into the dark" with everything else. That is the nature of this kind of waiting: "we *all* go" into it *all* the time.

When you have really looked with that greatly moral mind of waiting, and when no scrap of fear remains, then the silent funeral that we all go into is not at all a prophecy of doom or the dour outlook of an old, curmudgeonly poet.

To see the meaning of "we *all* go," is to realize the nature of universal salvation. To see the meaning of "we *all* go," is to realize that love is already the extant reality of sentient beings. There is nothing to escape from, nothing to attain. When you blow out the candle of fear, then your life fills up the whole universe, with nothing left out. This is what master Yunmen meant when he said "The kitchen pantry and the main gate." These things are not limited in space and time if you let go of the self. Just have the same faith as the pantry, or the floor, or the moon, or a cardboard box. When you abide in this faith, then you enter the darkness of "nobody's funeral." This is darkness that is beyond compare. It is light as well. Please realize this light in all that you do.

> Play the possum long enough,
> And you'll soon tire of the game.
> Seeking dawn, head for dusk.
> Soft like the whisper of winter streams,
> It flows on endlessly through moonless nights.

1   Yu, Beogcheon. *The Great Circle: American Writers and the Orient.* First Edition. Detroit: Wayne State University Press, 1983. Print. 161.

2   Broughton, Jeffrey L. (trans). *The Chan Whip Anthology: A Companion to Zen Practice.* Oxford, 2015. Print. 94-95.

Seeing Straight

The Sultan of Savoir

Wallace Stevens' "The Plain Sense of Things"

Expressing 80 percent of it is a feat unto itself, like catching the sultan's arrow with your teeth. Biting down, how can you express the remaining 20 percent?

The Plain Sense of Things

After the leaves have fallen, we return
To a plain sense of things. It is as if
We had come to an end of the imagination,
Inanimate in an inert savoir.

It is difficult even to choose the adjective
For this blank cold, this sadness without cause.
The great structure has become a minor house.
No turban walks across the lessened floors.

The greenhouse never so badly needed paint.
The chimney is fifty years old and slants to one side.
A fantastic effort has failed, a repetition
In a repetitiousness of men and flies.

Yet the absence of the imagination had
Itself to be imagined. The great pond,
The plain sense of it, without reflections, leaves,
Mud, water like dirty glass, expressing silence

Of a sort, silence of a rat come out to see,
The great pond and its waste of the lilies, all this
Had to be imagined as an inevitable knowledge,
Required, as a necessity requires.

(1954)

Robert Aitken, Roshi, in his wonderful essay about "The Snow Man," by Wallace Stevens (1879–1955), explained that the poet had on one occasion affirmed the influence of Buddhism on his work and in another place denied it.[1] Nevertheless, Stevens spent a great deal of time in contemplation, especially on his daily walks to and from work at the Hartford Insurance Company. His poems reflect a profound insight into the ever-changing "weathers" of the phenomenal world—the meat and potatoes of Zen practice—and I think he was at his best when he tried to express the essential, or intrinsic, reality of that world: the "plain sense of things."

Of course, there is a certain irony in a poem that seeks to explain the "plain sense of things" with language that is anything but plain. Most readers, for example, must resort to a dictionary to learn that "savoir" means a kind of ineffable knowing, but that hardly helps explain how such knowing might be "inert." And gaining access to the meaning of a line like "No turban walks across the lessened floor" is anyone's guess. Still, Stevens' very imaginative language points up just how difficult it is to really get a foothold in "the plain sense of things." It is beyond behavioral modesty and materially humble standards of living. It cannot be attained while the imaginative use of thought and language continues. The human effort to realize it, therefore, will always appear somewhat absurd, out of place, exotic, or foreign. So the poem cries out, in the only voice it can, to be returned to the primordial state that lies beyond the "end of the imagination."

Yet the "end of the imagination" is not a literal possibility. If the practice of Zen can teach you anything, it is that human fantasies are inexhaustible. But when the mind is still in the practice of *zazen* (seated meditation), "the absence of the imagination" can "itself be imagined." In that state, one may suddenly recognize the inherent limitations of thought. This sudden recognition might be tantamount to the experience of *kensho*, a glimpse of enlightenment.

It is important to understand, however, that kensho is not an experience in the usual sense. That is, it is not something that you add to your life history. It is more like a "non-experience"—a letting go of the mental clutter that has been obstructing your view.

When the multitude of delusions born of greed, anger, and ignorance drop away, it is as if "the leaves have fallen" and your view of the sky is suddenly unobstructed. You are presented with an open, unencumbered vision of reality in its pure, undefiled, "plain" sense. It is not that you have made things "plain" (that is the job of the imagination), but that you "return" to a view of the original nature that has always been before you.

Moment-By-Moment Returning

We return many times in the course of our years of practice to this plain sense of things. We also return moment by moment. But you should know that from the perspective of "the plain sense of things," this returning is not a movement from one place to another, or from one state of being to another. It is only that, in quieting the noise of *samsara* (the turbulence of self-clinging), you return to the brink of the "inert savoir"—that ineffable knowledge of reality's pure, infinite sky. We call this realization of openness *sunyata*, or emptiness. Because human conditioning runs so deep, however, you will have to return, time and again, to the awareness in which the "leaves have fallen."

If you do this enough, you eventually discover that the leaves are always falling, moment after moment, and they have always been doing this. They continuously fall from the trees of your conditioning, whether you realize it or not. But there is still more to see. You can see that leaves fall from leaves, trees fall from trees, and the sky falls away from the sky. Beyond this, falling itself continuously falls away. Rare and precious, this understanding is the understanding of your intrinsic state of absolute freedom. Seeing it clearly, you must then work to bring this understanding back into the realm of the imagination where it takes the form of wisdom and compassion.

Shakyamuni Buddha also returned many times. When he returned to his companions in the forest after his great awakening under the Bo tree, he did not call himself Siddhartha, or one who has returned, or even "the Buddha." He called himself the "Thus Come One." To have become the "Thus Come One," required him first to be the "Thus Gone One." At no time, however, has the Buddha ever come, or gone, anywhere.

To understand this, look around your room. See the objects in your room and notice their nature just as they are—that is, in "the plainest sense" that you can. What is the plain sense of the chair you're sitting in? What is the plain sense of the floor, the coffee cup, the desk, and so on? As you consider these objects, do not become entangled with judgments, evaluations, or emotions about them. Strip away all extraneous, added ideas, concepts, or preconceived notions until these ordinary objects are mirrored in your mind as no more than appearances.

You may find your breath suddenly bated and the mind, while alert and aware, utterly still ("inanimate") in the midst of things. Penetrating further, you will eventually discover that, though you are hovering in the present moment of reality—keen, aware, luminous, courageous, and still—you no longer know things. The floor, the chair, the book, the cup, and so on cease to exist independently, even though they are present to the senses. Provisionally speaking, you could say that this is to be "Thus Gone." It is temporarily to relinquish the imagination. Reflecting this in your life then means expressing silence "of a sort," and this sort of silence is the path of the "inevitable knowledge" that liberates all sentient beings.

To acquire "inevitable knowledge" means to just be yourself, living in the present moment with perfect sincerity. To come into your life with that kind of immediacy and sincerity is to become the "Thus Come One." When you say "Thus," you are really saying "Buddha." Not Shakyamuni Buddha, but the primordial Buddha (which, in Zen, is Vairochana). Vairochana is the innate Buddha wisdom that is no different from your very life, right now, just as it is: thus.

When you say "Come," you are really saying "Dharma." This Dharma is not the law of causation, but *anuttara-samyak-sambodhi*, supreme, perfect, complete enlightenment. This means that though you may attain nirvana, you cannot remain within it. This is most mysterious and profound. To master that which is unattainable is to realize that it is already innately your life as it is.

When you say "One," you are really understanding that Buddha and Dharma are fused into a single, complete, and harmonious reality. This harmony can be called *Sangha*, but in this context it is not the Buddhist community. If you could stand exactly where two sides of a coin meet, you might be aware of "sides" and simultaneously aware of "meet." This is "One." So when you say "Thus Come One," you really mean that you and all beings and things are awakened simultaneously throughout all space and time. The Thus Come One is the Three Treasures of Buddha, Dharma, and Sangha as one body.

Almost Not Losing Yourself

As Stevens came near the end of his life, he began to realize that the "supreme effort" he had mustered as a poet would never produce the fundamental, ineffable nature of reality, "the plain sense of things" that he wanted so much to realize. He was forced to admit that, though he had come close, the universe remained just out of reach. Vast and beautiful and lush as his poetic accomplishments were, he had failed to *say* it with all the immediacy with which he felt it. His work was no more successful than the work of any other imaginative person, his poetry but "a repetition / In a repetitiousness of men and flies." The Sultan of Savoir took off the turban of his sovereign reign. A "fantastic effort had failed."

In Case 46 of *The Blue Cliff Record*, a similar fantastic effort failed. In this case, master Jingqing Daofu (863–937) suddenly asked a monk, "What's that sound outside the gate?"

His monk answered, "That's the voice of the rain."

Just this much is worth thinking about. Everyone knows the sound of rain, so why did Jingqing ask about it? In his commentary on this koan, master Xuedou Chongxian (980–1052) writes, "He casually lets down a hook. He doesn't suffer from deafness." This means that Jingqing is fishing for a worthy student with a subtle test.

For his part, the monk knows that *everyone* knows what rain sounds like. So why does he even bother answering Jingqing?

Because that's what we do. When the teacher speaks, we reply. Every word must be strained through until we reach the plain sense of it. Even though the monk has words, his words have no sound. He is really quite a capable fellow.

Jingqing then turned the conversation in a new direction, saying, "People are all turned upside down. They lose themselves and chase after things."

Hearing this, the monk asked, "What about you, Teacher?"

Jingqing said, "I almost don't lose myself."

The monk asked, "What do you mean 'I almost don't lose myself'?"

Jingqing replied, "it's pretty easy to get the fundamental point but to say the whole thing is difficult."

What is the "fantastic effort" that has failed here? Has the teacher failed to express the "plain sense" of the sound of the rain drops? You see, he's trying to include both "form"—the experiential side of the sound of rain—*and* "emptiness"—the intrinsic side of the sound of rain, which has no characteristics at all. A great deal of your practice of Zen will be about seeing this intrinsic side, even though it is not something you can see with your eyes or access with words. Just to get a good glimpse of it is hard to do.

And once you see it, you will need to express it in an original, authentic way. Since the intrinsic side has no characteristics at all, "it will be difficult even to choose the adjective" that would describe the plain sense of the sound of rain, or of a book, or of the dog barking next door. Fortunately, the Zen tradition therefore has usually resorted to figurative language to indirectly point to this intrinsic nature. Coincidentally, many of Zen's tropes for the intrinsic side—such as autumn, frost, winter, cold, and ice—are found in Stevens' poems. In "The Plain Sense of Things," emptiness is "this blank cold," the still and chilly air of a New England autumn.

A Board-Carrying Fellow

To see reality clearly, then, means not only having your own personal insight into emptiness, but expressing it *completely* without adding or removing anything. It can take a lifetime of diligent practice to be able to do this with spontaneous clarity.

Each time you try to "return / to a plain sense of things," you will discover, as Stevens did, that "the great structure" of your supreme effort to become the master of your life "has become a minor house." A flaw can be found in every construction of the truth because there is no end to the imagination. And there you are: "The greenhouse never so badly needed paint. / The chimney is fifty years old and slants to one side." Your "fantastic effort has failed"; whatever you say will be an utterance that "slants to one side." As the great master Xuedou wrote, "If your whole body were an ear, you still wouldn't be able to hear it. If your whole body were a mouth, you still wouldn't be able to speak of it. If your whole body were mind, you still wouldn't be able to perceive it."[2]

But not all is disappointment. Your very failure is a necessity of practice. If you do not try, in spite of the inevitable failure, then you cannot see how to deepen and clarify your spiritual insight.

Once, when I was first beginning to be serious about Zen practice, I thought I had had an important "experience" during zazen. So I wrote a letter to my teacher, explaining my "insight," explaining that it felt as though my vision was as clear as that of a soaring eagle. He wrote back with the inevitable, crushing news that, though I was progressing, my understanding was *nothing* like that of a soaring eagle, or for that matter, even a pigeon flopping around on the ground. It was, he wrote, "like that of a cow."

But it was important for me to learn that. And for years afterwards, I had to hear that I was sticking to one side or the other, no matter how hard I tried to pin down the "plain sense of things." I was (and I still am), what the Zen tradition calls "a board-carrying fellow." This is a traditional Zen way of referring to someone with a lopsided view of things. A person who carries a board over the shoulder can only see to one side. I have been carrying that board for so long that it has worn a notch in my shoulder. Now I switch shoulders. And I try to help my students with their boards too.

So we are never done with our practice; it is an endless road of trying to imagine "the absence of the imagination." More than once, my teacher, Myoyu Andersen, Roshi, said, "You know what to do; just keep going." That statement conveys both the reality and the necessity. It's really such a simple thing: just observe and accept the truth of what you see, of what you are. As you penetrate ever deeper into her statement, you will always find "an inevitable knowledge" at the root of it. You simply can't avoid it. It's like the ground or the air. So even as your insight is deepened and clarified, you come to learn that that knowledge was inevitable. So too is your failure to express the "plain sense of things."

This inevitable process of failure and clarification is subtly reflected in Stevens' poem, in the objective correlative of the speaker's changing focus of attention. It moves from "the great structure" of delusion to the greenhouse, the semi-transparent realm of emptiness that borders "the plain sense of things." As clear as it is, the greenhouse too is a dissatisfying architecture of the imagination; it "never so badly needed paint." Clarification and failure are followed by further clarification as the speaker's awareness shifts again to "the great pond, / The plain sense of it, without reflections"—a view of reality that does not add something to it or take something away from it. The "mud, water like dirty glass, expressing silence" can then be seen as a metaphor for insight that would fit right into the classic Zen texts of ancient China. And yet even this silence is *still* only "silence / Of a sort." The vision is still incomplete.

In Case 89 of *The Blue Cliff Record*,[3] Yunyan Tansheng (780–841) asked Daowu Yuanzhi (769–835), "What does the Bodhisattva of Great Compassion use so many hands and eyes for?"

This question is based on the traditional iconography of Kanzeon Bodhisattva, the archetypal figure of compassion, who has 84,000 thousand arms and eyes with which she helps all sentient beings toward enlightenment.

To this Daowu responded, "It's like someone asleep reaching back for a pillow in the middle of the night."

Yunyan said, "I understand."

Daowu said, "How do you understand it?"

Yunyan said, "All over the body are hands and eyes."

Daowu said, "You have said quite a bit there, but you've only said eighty percent of it."

Yunyan said, "What do you say, Elder Brother?"

Daowu, said, "Throughout the body are hands and eyes."

These two men were Dharma brothers, but they were also biological brothers. Their exchange is a wonderful example of "brotherly love." Each one is trying to help the other and to help himself attain the deepest, clearest realization possible. Do you think that one of them has the upper-hand? And how does the statement, "It's like someone asleep reaching back for a pillow in the middle of the night" come to 80 percent of the truth? Do you think that Daowu's statement, "Throughout the body are hands and eyes" says it all, 100 percent?

As I mentioned above, the great master Xuedou said, "If your whole body were a mouth, you still wouldn't be able to speak of it." He went on, however, to give us a clue about how to understand this towering koan. He said, "Without a mouth, how would you speak? Without a mind, how would you perceive? Here, if you can unfurl a single pathway, then you'd be a fellow student with the ancient Buddhas."

Can you see that pathway out of lopsided views, views that stick to one side or another, views that are incomplete? If you speak, you wreck it; if you keep silent, you fail. What is the way out of this that will give you one hundred percent of "the plain sense of things"?

Just Keep Going

The master Nanquan (748–834) once said, "The Buddhas of the past, present, and future don't see it. Cats and cows see it." What cats and cows see is not different from what you and I see, but I'm pretty sure they don't talk about. To see the nature of your life like a cat, a cow, or "a rat come out to see / the great pond" is to bring things down to about as close as most of us can ever hope "to a plain sense of things." "The great pond" of the last stanza of Stevens' poem is nothing other than the self "without reflections." The rat sees it because the rat lives there, naturally, spontaneously, harmoniously. The "waste of the lilies" have been locked in a sheet of October ice. "All this," Stevens writes, "had to be imagined as an inevitable knowledge."

To understand this "inevitable knowledge" is to realize the real significance of Myoyu Roshi's "You know what to do; just keep going." When you just keep going, then the work of Bodhisattvas is actualized. Bodhisattvas are the enlightened beings who postpone their own ultimate perfection in nirvana until all other sentient beings proceed through the gates of the Dharma first.

It is also to realize the "plain sense of things." This is the way that wisdom arises from wisdom, and compassion arises from compassion. It is the same realization that Kashyapa had at the moment when Shakyamuni Buddha twirled a flower on Mount Grdhrakatu 2500 years ago. Kashyapa had seen the "plain sense of" that flower, and of himself. When this happened, he returned to the Buddha, and to all sentient beings. And he smiled. It was not an entirely silent moment of face-to-face understanding, but there was "silence / Of a sort." It has nothing to do with Kashyapa not using words. Seeing Kashyapa's smile, the Buddha spoke, and he said, "I have the Treasury of the Eye of the True Dharma and Wondrous Mind of Nirvana, and this I transmit to the Great Kashyapa."

You may think, therefore, that the plain sense of things has something to do with being spontaneous or that it is something like "being here now." If you think that way, then that is not it at all. That is just thinking. Of this kind of understanding, the Japanese master Keizan Jokin (1268–1325) wrote in *The Transmission of Light*, "Even if contrivance ends, there is still some preservation of the self; if you are like this you make the mistake of falling into the deep pit of liberation, so this state has always been called religious attachment."[4]

But even if you are certain beyond all doubt that you have surpassed all inadequacies, you will still have a flaw. Do you see it? It's OK if you do. It's OK if you don't. Your "seeing" or your "not seeing" is inevitable. Because it is inevitable, there is nothing you can do about it. Sickness and medicine cure each other. When there is nothing you can do about it, what then is the "plain sense of things"? How do you expose the reality of there being nothing you can do about it?

Shall I make it easier for you? Just relax amid your failure, and show me, now, without any shillyshally: how do you keep going after you return to "the plain sense of things"?

> Having seen through autumn trees,
> He catches sight of his ancestral home,
> Inevitably wandering familiar, empty rooms.

From doors left open to the cold,
He watches lilies blooming in the ice.

1   Aitken, Robert. *Original Dwelling Place: Zen Buddhist Essays*. Berkeley: Counterpoint, 1997. Print. 188.

2   J. C. Cleary, Thomas Cleary. *The Blue Cliff Record*. Boston: Shambhala, 1992. Print. 489.

3   Ibid.

4   Keizan, Zen M. *Transmission of Light (Denkoroku): Zen in the Art of Enlightenment*. Trans. Thomas Cleary. San Francisco: North Point Press, 1990. Print. 148.

Incapable of Tears

H.D.'s "Sea Rose"

Inhaling, you smell nothing. Grabbing, you get pricked. Why must you go on suffering so?
If you want to make a silk purse out of sow's ear, or a mirror out of a tile, your whole life
must drip through these acrid petals.

Sea Rose

Rose, harsh rose,
marred and with stint of petals,
meagre flower, thin,
sparse of leaf,

more precious
than a wet rose
single on a stem—
you are caught in the drift.

Stunted, with small leaf,
you are flung on the sand,
you are lifted
in the crisp sand
that drives in the wind.

Can the spice rose
drip such acrid fragrance
hardened in a leaf?

(1916)

"Sea Rose" by H.D. (1886–1961) is a wonderful representation of the kind of concentrated awareness that might be cultivated were we willing to walk a while along this poem's shores. It hovers in the present moment, it sees things as they really are—but certainly not in the way that many of us would have them. Indeed, the rose before you now is probably not the rose of your desire. Blasted by driving winds and saltwater spray, "stunted, with small leaf / ... [and] flung on the sand," this rose may be admirable for having survived its harsh environment, but it has nothing of the glory of a "wet rose / single on a stem" that glows in the florist's chilled display case. No, the sea rose is a tough old thing, "lifted" only to be "flung" down again on the "crisp sand" of its own disgrace, so unlike the rose that is the very spirit of passion, perfection, and harmony. Handed a dozen of those, would you not instinctively cradle them as you would a baby, reflexively dipping your nose into their midst? Even when you know that years of hybridization have robbed them of their scent, you sniff them anyway; you sense the heavenly fragrance of serenity.

What, then, makes the sea rose, this little rag of a plant, "more precious" than the rose you'd offer a friend? Forced to confront its "harsh," "marred" "stint of petals," you have to set aside your hothouse dreams and bathe your eyes in another kind of beauty. It is the beauty, not of the sight, but of seeing itself—a distinction that H.D. and other Imagist poets learned when they "bowed to winds from the East,"[1] studying the Buddhist-influenced poetry of China and Japan, grafting certain "Zen" perspectives onto their writing, almost without their knowing it. And, in H.D.'s case, there was the study of *Light on the Path*,[2] a Theosophical Society publication that purported to give instruction in "eastern wisdom." She owned several copies and heavily annotated them. As a prelude to granting access to its esoteric pages, the author of *Light on the Path* made it plain that one must be prepared to change. "Before the eyes can see," he wrote, "they must be incapable of tears." It was a notion that nicely paralleled the Zen perspective on the often unrecognized link between the processes of perception and human suffering.

To find out what makes this rose "more precious," then, means making sure you don't rush past it from the get-go, thinking it unworthy of your time and attention. Fortunately, H.D.'s poem helps us slow down the processes of perception and awareness. It does this through its sound and its syntax, both of which reflect the affective quality of mindfulness meditation. The absence of verbs in the first stanza, for example, immediately creates a kind of stilled state of awareness in which the mind can "just be," allowing it to fully attend to the immediate surroundings. Blunt monosyllables drum against the shore of each line, creating a wave-like, lulling effect. You can hear that surf in the "r" and "m" sounds of "rose," "marred," "meagre," and "sparse" as they launch each line of the first stanza, wave after wave.

Rose, harsh rose,
marred and with stint of petals,
meagre flower, thin,
sparse of leaf,

As your concentration increases on the rose, the pounding surf grows less conspic-
uous; the stressed syllables naturally recede to more relaxed locations in the middle
and at the ends of the lines:

more **precious**
than a **wet** rose
single on a **stem**—
you are **caught** in the drift.

Stunted, with small leaf,
you are **flung** on the sand,
you are **lifted**
in the **crisp sand**
that **drives** in the **wind**.

H.D.'s meticulous use of words has created a poetry of *samadhi*, or single-pointed concentration that alters your perception of it. Having stopped long enough to actually look
at this bedraggled little plant, you suddenly become aware of how familiar its "acrid
fragrance" is. It is the scent of your life. It is *your* life that roars with the surf of impermanence and change. It is *your* world that is studded with blemished, imperfect things.

When I think about all the things I've failed to do—play the guitar, build a house,
have washboard abs, travel to outer space—I suffer. I don't want to look at my what-
might-have-beens. I feel bad seeing the buds of ambition that were "flung on the sand,"
left "Stunted" and "sparse of leaf." But to follow the Buddha Way is to examine the
nature of *dukkha*, or suffering. This requires patience with unpleasant experiences, whether it is a snarl of a rose or the death of a loved one. Dwelling on the shore
of unlikable things is the face of practice. I once knew a man who took this idea to
the extreme. He practiced meditation while sitting on a bench in a city park. There,
under the green and lovely trees, and with the sound of children happily playing near-
by, he made a practice of dredging up the worst possible thing that he could think of.
Spending time with his imaginary nightmares allowed him to see all the way through
his perceptions to the root condition by which suffering can be ended.

So the poem's closing question, "Can the spice rose / drip such acrid fragrance /
hardened in a leaf?" is the Zen shore that beckons us beyond our hothouse dreams. I

have the sense that this question is meant rhetorically; it is the "negative capability" of the sea rose that H.D. wants to reveal. To see suffering as she does is not a matter of wallowing in our——or the world's——imperfections, but of seeing what *is*.

That means, in part, to become aware of the actual process of "seeing." From the Buddhist perspective, "seeing" (as well as hearing, smelling, tasting touching, and thinking) is a rather complex psychological process involving form, sensation, perception, discrimination, and awareness. *Form* refers to material objects (including thought objects and the physical body) that are apprehended by our sense organs. *Sensation* is experience in its most fundamental aspect——as pleasant, unpleasant, or neutral. *Perception* is that part of awareness that categorizes experience according to the sense organ that perceives it. Perception is also responsible for judging pleasant, unpleasant, and neutral experiences as such——which in turn leads to motivation for action. *Discrimination* is the process of mind that formulates ideas and feelings about experience, on the basis of which we act. *Awareness* is consciousness in a general sense; it is the sense organ of "thought objects," and it also encompasses the activities of sensation, perception, and discrimination. Together, these functions, known as the *skandhas*, are what constitute a "self," and all of them are empty, devoid of any enduring quality.

It is generally not possible to detect the steps in this sequence directly. But when the mind is very composed, centered, and focused, it is possible to reflect upon the process by which we categorize sensory information, respond to it, and act upon it, (usually) with some form of attachment to the desired outcome. What we notice is the lightning speed by which the bucket brigade of consciousness operates. (The mind's sheer processing speed suggests, among other things, that trying to control it would be very hard to do.) If I am looking at H.D.'s rose, light enters my eye at 186,000 miles per second, producing a *sensation*. The upside-down picture of the rose on my retina is turned right-side up in my brain, producing a *perception*, and this perception is reflexively categorized as (in this case) "unpleasant"——because it doesn't conform to my idea of a "beautiful" rose.

At that point, the process of *discrimination* begins, and I start formulating ideas and feelings about the ugliness of this rose. Then I act. I make a decision to walk away from it. I don't like it. If I see a lot of such roses on this particular mental beach, I will dislike the beach. If this beach is where I am spending my vacation, I will come home feeling disappointed about my vacation in an ugly place. All of this may arise from a picture of an ugly rose acquired in a fraction of a second.

This might not be much of a problem if life were as simple as avoiding a known set of miserable-looking flowers. But when the thorn of unpleasantness is a divorce, bad weather, losing a job, getting sick, or the death of loved one, it's a different story. It is a different story when the perceptions and discriminations of the girls at the prom motivate them to shun the overweight guy standing by the punch bowl. When they do that, suffering arises—for them and for that boy—at 186,000 miles per second.

In a state of meditative awareness, however, the process of seeing can be temporarily suppressed at the level of, say, *perception*. Or, perhaps more accurately, meditation can *temporarily suspend* the activity of discrimination by which we form ideas and judgments in accordance with our preferences—preferences which produce suffering for ourselves and others. When we engage in this kind of practice with sincerity and regularity, however, we begin to notice patterns—places in our cognitive processing where we tend to stick, to be uncomfortable, to habitually make a problem for ourselves. Given enough experience (and aided by a good teacher), it is possible to keep our minds so tightly focused on, say, H.D.'s sea rose, *that only the present moment* of its existence can be perceived. The conceptualizations that would otherwise distort our understanding do not arise. We see the rose as it is.

In other words, when the "acrid fragrance" of the sea rose is "hardened" in meditative consciousness, it renders the eye "incapable of tears." This is not yet quite the end of suffering, but it is at least a temporary refuge from discriminating judgments. This aware, alert, but equanimous form of concentration is fixed in the present moment—a fact that is nicely underscored by H.D.'s use of the present tense. The mind of the present moment is the mind of paying attention to what is. Thus, the choice we face is between suffering and paying attention, between tears and being "incapable of tears."

It is hard to accept such a proposition. For most of us, suffering appears to be an intermittent experience—like cow pies in life's field of daisies. The beauty of "Sea Rose," (and meditation!) though, is that it challenges this view of suffering. It suggests, as did the Buddha, that the end of suffering is not a matter of avoiding it in the same way you might mince your way through a field of cow pies, while intermittently picking daisies. It is, rather, a matter of seeing your life as nothing but suffering. If you think the prospect of seamless suffering is too much to bear, then consider this: to think that suffering is a "sometimes" thing means thinking of its opposite—happiness or contentedness—is also a "sometimes" thing. If that's how you view things, then half of your life will be stunted by dissatisfaction, and the other half, while initially pleasant, will eventually produce dissatisfaction when it comes to an end. Think about how much wiser it would be to see both hothouse roses and roses by the sea as equals—as moments of your life that are neither inherently pleasant nor unpleasant but simply how things are. When you see things this way, you start to see that your whole life—not just the parts that gratify you—are a reason for gratitude and joy.

The master Mazu Daiyi (709–788) was one who certainly saw all the way through his suffering by suffering completely. He once became seriously ill. While he was recovering in the infirmary, the head priest came to see him and pay his respects.

"How are you feeling today, master?" asked the priest.

Mazu replied, "Sun-faced Buddha, Moon-faced Buddha."

Mazu's answer is one of the most famous statements in the Zen tradition. If you had been there, what would you have said in reply to Mazu?

Some years ago, I spent days in bed with the flu. My fever reached over 103 degrees. I couldn't move. My body hurt so bad that I thought I would die. I couldn't even get up to get a drink of water. I never want to be that sick again. To me, that was some pretty terrible suffering. If the priest of this koan had asked me how I was feeling then, I think I could only have groaned. But Mazu says, "Sun-faced Buddha, Moon-faced Buddha." Two Buddhas, two different faces. What does Mazu mean? How do these two Buddhas explain how he feels? And how does his answer help us understand the suffering of H.D.'s rose?

It might help a little if I tell you that these Buddhas are described in a scripture. The scripture says that the Sun-faced Buddha lives for 1800 years. That's a really long time to shine so beautifully in the sky! The Moon-faced Buddha, by contrast, lives for one day and one night. Compared to the Sun-faced Buddha, the life of the Moon-faced Buddha is over in the blink of an eye. Of those two Buddhas, which one would you rather be? Which one do you think suffers more? The raging, burning Sun-faced Buddha, or the cold, dark, Moon-faced Buddha? They are both Buddhas, so why would they suffer at all?

If you want to answer this koan, then you will have to "drip such acrid fragrance" through your life that the only thing left is Mazu's illness or my flu. When you see all the way through Mazu's suffering, you cure him. When Mazu is cured, then you know the Sun-faced Buddha and the Moon-faced Buddha as yourself.

To see the "more precious" rose in the sickly sea rose, then, you must see the sea rose with great skill. There is no hidden perfection somewhere "inside" the rose that you need to find. It is just that its causeless, unborn nature, perceived with the wise mind of Buddha, is already apparent in its very condition. To see the unborn nature of the rose or Mazu's illness is the end of suffering. It is to know "stunted" without shame, "meagre" without sorrow, "small of leaf" without despair. Unhindered by the discriminating mind, the rose is saved—and so are you. Just look dispassionately at anything, and you'll see exactly what I mean.

I cannot over-emphasize how important this aspect of Zen practice is. Without it, your response to the sea roses of your life will stop at pity, which presumes that you are somehow different, somehow "above" their lowly stations in the sand. Without practice, you might achieve a kind of sympathy with the rose, recognizing that there are similarities between its imperfections and your own. But that recognition, no matter how comforting it may be, is not the end of suffering. In fact, that recognition, all by itself, may exacerbate your suffering.

But when you wholeheartedly devote yourself to practice, you can walk through the doors of hell without blinking an eye. When you are clear and calm and mindfully focused, there is neither life nor death, even as you are born and die. You are just here with your coffee, cold in the cup that is chipped and cracked. You no longer put a head on top of your head, desperately trying to add something to life to make it come out right. It's already right.

If you practice hard, you will discover that the world in which sentient beings suffer is not one of a two-world system—one world in which we prick our fingers and another world in which roses have no thorns. It is to enter the realm of compassion. Compassion means to "suffer with." You should not be fooled into thinking that your feelings of sympathy for others' unhappiness is compassion. Real compassion is most rare. It is not accessible from imperfection and suffering. It is only accessible from the sea rose, or cold pizza, or your lack of washboard abs. It cannot be attained by the adoption of an attitude or a philosophy (which Yasutani Roshi once defined as "the study of delusion"). Anything that preserves a semblance of callousness, aloofness, or the arrogance of "transcendence" will not reach this realm. To just be right here, right now, with no regrets or ulterior motives, to apprehend the unknowable mind of the present, is to suddenly see the 84,000 arms of Kanzeon Bodhisattva (the deity of compassion) sprouting from your shoulders. It is to weep the acrid tears of sentient beings everywhere, washing away their suffering and their despair.

Just see that the world as it is, without anything added to it or taken away from it, is a totality that is all you're ever going to get. The world as it is cannot be other than *this*. Because it cannot be other than *this*, it is complete. Being a complete world, it must be a perfect world. To arrive in its midst, just enter through the gate of broken cups and dog poop, loneliness and hurt, stained rugs and terrible coffee. Then you will see how much more fun and interesting things are! Look! Look! Everything is broken! Everything is ugly!

> When you are in bloom,
> Then the Way is not the Way
> And therefore it's the Way.
> In the light of the noon-day sun,
> Spring flowers pile up to the heavens.

1   Beinecke Rare Book & Manuscript Library, Yale. "Harriet Monroe and the 'Imagists.'" *Petals on a Wet Black Bough: American Modernist Writers and the Orient.* 1997. Web. 19 June 2015.

2   Beinecke Rare Book & Manuscript Library, Yale University. "H.D., Amy Lowell and John Gould Fletcher." Exhibition. *Petals on a Wet Black Bough: American Modernist Writers and the Orient*. 1997. Web. 19 June 2015.

White Chickens All the Way Down

William Carlos Williams' "The Red Wheelbarrow"

The Master of the Glimpse has troubled himself to build a floorless, nine-story pagoda just to make a point that everyone already understands. Asking how to enter—it's perfectly obvious. As for leaving it, no one has ever managed to do it.

The Red Wheelbarrow

so much depends
upon

a red wheel
barrow

glazed with rain
water

beside the white
chickens.

(1923)

Given its brevity—and what appears to be a lack of anything important to say—"The Red Wheelbarrow," by Williams Carlos Williams (1883–1963), does not advertise itself as a particularly difficult or subtle poem. In fact, my literature students often dismiss it. For them, it is cereal without milk, a door without a knob. It is nothing more than a glimpse of a moment that passed nearly a century ago in the backyard of Williams' neighbor, Thaddeus Lloyd Marshall.[1]

Since then, this mere sliver of a poem has defied mere classroom explanations. Many have taken a firm grip of its handles, expecting to make short work of it, only to find that they couldn't lift them. Like Excalibur or the robe of the sixth Zen Patriarch (See my essay "Light-Years Away From It" for a wonderful legend about this amazing teacher), that red wheelbarrow remains the immovable artifact of our American literary backyard. Complete unto itself, in want of nothing and giving just the same, the red wheelbarrow neither comes nor goes, but stands its ground, obdurate as it is elusive, ordinary as it is ineffable.

So what does it mean? Why did Williams write it?

To answer those questions, you must enter into the poem with your whole life. If you can do that, then you will understand why the red wheelbarrow endures as an object lesson in perception that is hardly different from any Zen koan. You will discover—just as one of my Buddhist friends did many years ago—that there is a reason why Williams' poem remains such an important spiritual legacy. You will discover that you have already lifted the old, worn handles, and that the red wheelbarrow, in all its humble simplicity, has rolled forth with the momentum of the universe. Then, as my friend put it, you will be struck, "as if by lightning."

A Box and its Lid

Few of us will have such an experience on the first reading of the poem. Most of us must doggedly pursue the red wheelbarrow to discern its meaning. If you approach it as a koan, you will have to live with it for a time, imaginatively pushing it around the green lawns of your mind, meticulously watching it list to the left and right as you waddle around with its ungainly weight before you. You work it.

Clearly, Williams wanted us to have just that kind of experience. He took pains to design the poem so that it would reflect the nature of seeing, then lifting and pushing, a wheelbarrow. Each stanza starts with a three-word line, like a wheelbarrow at rest on three points. Then it moves, rolling along on just one. It rests again on three, rolls again on one, stanza by stanza. Even the placement of the lines of each stanza on the page appear as silhouettes of wheelbarrows. Given the enjambed line breaks, reading the poem aloud can evoke the physical jerk and wobble of the gait of one whose wheelbarrow is full. A certain careening joy could be taken in this—could be, that is, until you start questioning the subtle peculiarities of the poem.

For example, you may notice that the wheelbarrow is "beside the white / chickens," a reversal of our normal tendency to prioritize animate things in relation to inanimate ones. Who would not more naturally point out that the white chickens are beside the red wheelbarrow? And to ensure there is no mistake about what constitutes the intended focal point, Williams adds that the wheelbarrow is "glazed with rain / water," a lovely elaboration which reminds us that this is no generic garden tool but a unique specimen, momentarily glimpsed. And, finally, there is the understated remark that this ordinary thing, this old, red, beat-up wheelbarrow, is seemingly the *one* thing that "so much depends / upon." You can hardly avoid asking yourself *What is it* that depends upon the red wheelbarrow?

What is it indeed?

It's as though Williams thinks the answer to his question is so obvious that it's not worth mentioning. He provides no help. So the question nags at you. What—what *exactly*—"depends / upon" a red wheelbarrow? There are obvious choices—like sand, manure, old leaves, chicken feed, or sticks—they depend on the wheelbarrow to be transported here and there. Maybe this poem is all about the future of the farm, or the beauty of a backyard. Maybe that red wheelbarrow is all about some kind of land-owner's glorying in his prized real estate. But I don't think so.

If what you want out of this poem is insight into the human condition—and that is what Williams wanted—then you have no choice but to try to imagine ever-bigger, more important things that might "depend / upon" that red wheelbarrow. You have to want more. You need more. So, even if it's a stretch, you have to try-on lots of possibilities, sizing up each one for an instinctive sense of whether it works or not. Sometimes it's hard to know. I remember asking about this as a novice in koan practice. How do you know if you have the right answer to a koan? I was told then what I'll tell you now: the answer to a koan will fit the koan as a lid fits a box. Working on a koan, then, is like going through a room full of lids, trying one after the other until you find one that fits the box just perfectly.

Sometimes you go through all the lids in the room only to discover that none of them fit. But the frustration you feel at this is a positive sign of progress. It means that you've exhausted all the easy intellectual answers, all the things that Williams thought clouded our judgement. Your work on the koan can then begin again with greater penetration, examining that box until you see it as your life. What do you depend upon? What depends upon you? If you study the matter with sufficient focus, you eventually discover that you've been holding the missing lid that fits the box all along. You just didn't realize it. It's like looking all through the house for your car keys, only to discover you were holding them in your hand.

Can you follow the same process now with "The Red Wheelbarrow"? The central image of the poem seems strangely incomplete. Your quick answers about garden work or property management just don't fit. If you continue to pile such intellectual responses on top of one another, the red wheelbarrow of your life will remain too heavy to move. You can lift, but your back will stay bent. You can push, but your feet will stay planted. When you start to relinquish the idea that any particular answer is going to work, then the words "So much / depends" begin to sound an awful lot like "*everything* depends." And if everything depends upon a red wheelbarrow, then that red wheelbarrow must be a lot more important than it seems. It must be the center of the whole universe.

Such a Clever Young Man!

There is a funny story about this ultimate form of dependency that has appeared, in various versions, for at least two hundred years. In one version, a learned scientist gave a public lecture on the structure of the heavenly bodies, explaining that the Earth orbits the sun, and that the sun is just one of trillions of suns in the Milky Way galaxy. In turn, the Milky Way is just one of billions upon billions of galaxies in an infinite, and infinitely expanding, universe. "All this," said the scientist with a sweep of his hand at the end of his talk, "suggests that the Earth is not fixed in space or time and can by no means be considered the center of the universe. In fact," he said momentously, "*there is no center at all. Nothing at all is fixed.*"

Thunderous applause.

People began to leave the lecture hall, giddy with various conjectures about the meaning of life without a center. The scientist was just then squaring up his sheaf of notes when an elderly woman approached him and said, "You seem like a very well educated young man," she began. "But I'm afraid you're mistaken about the Earth not being fixed in space."

"How am I mistaken?" he asked.

"Well," the old woman replied, "the world is flat. And what's more, it rests on the back of a giant turtle."

Hearing this, the scientist smirked and said, "In that case, madam, on what does this giant turtle rest?"

"Oh, you think you're such a clever young man!" scoffed the old woman. "Everyone knows that it's turtles *all the way down!*"

This has become the hilarious punchline of the infinite regression theory of the universe. But while we may laugh at the naiveté of an old woman, the fact is that most of us are just like her. We don't translate our "scientific" understanding into logical actions in our lives. We are "so very clever" that we believe, on the one hand, that nothing is fixed. On the other hand, we don't hesitate to assert that we are "right," and others "wrong"—that some things make common sense and others do not. When push comes to shove, we stand our "ground," even though that ground does not "depend upon" anything at all.

We believe, in other words, that it's turtles all the way down.

Being Hungry Enough

Perhaps you will throw up your hands and walk away from imponderable discussions about wheelbarrows and turtles. But I hope you don't do that. There is more at stake here than you may realize, a matter of grave importance. For Williams, the importance of the matter lay in humanity's presumption that its own grand thoughts and views, its perspectives and cherished opinions, are something more than a delusion—what Williams called "a dialectic cloud" within which we are trapped.

A great koan, like Williams' "The Red Wheelbarrrow," however, will force you to question your common sense thinking, your cloud of delusive thought. The harder you try to give common sense answers to a question like *What exactly "depends upon" a red wheelbarrow?* the faster your common sense disappears in a haze of uncertainty. That experience changes the nature of the question. Penetrating deeper into it, you may notice yourself asking something simpler, something more direct, like *What is the red wheelbarrow?* But how can you answer that if everything you think you know is based on a fantasy turtle that is based on a fantasy turtle, "all the way down"? No matter what answer you come up with, it disintegrates in your hands.

In Case 37 of the *Blue Cliff Record*, master Panshan Baoji (720–814) tried to get at the heart of the matter. He said, "In the whole world, there is nothing at all—so where will you find the Mind?" This is one of the most famous statements ever made in the history of Zen. Panshan plumbed the depths and scraped the sky, looking for something he could depend upon. But like every adept before or since, he came up empty-handed. So he said, "there is nothing at all." Then he asked, "where will you find the Mind?" He meant *Where will you find any basis for your mind, your understanding, your thoughts and feelings?* If your mind has no basis, then what *are* your thoughts and feelings?

Should you shrug your shoulders and give up on the question? If you do that, then "The Red Wheelbarrow" will never mean anything and Williams shouldn't have bothered to write it. If you give up, then you too shouldn't bother to do anything! You shouldn't bother to get out of bed in the morning. But stay in bed sometime and see how long your resolve lasts. When you get hungry enough, or when you have to pee, believe me, you'll get out of bed. And right then and there, you'll be pushing that red wheelbarrow out the bedroom door.

A Bodhisattva from Hell

If you are, or want to be, the kind of person that Williams' was writing to, then you're going to have to discover the implications of Panshan's statement that there is nothing at all, nothing that you can depend upon that doesn't slip through the fingers of the infinite regression theory. You're going to have to discover where it *all* comes from, the Source of *everything*, the Source of the whole world. To attain the Source, you must be wise before you learn anything. You must be a diva before learning to sing.

If this baffles you, please don't be put off. I was baffled too, once upon a time, when I was given the koan "What is the Source?" That koan is a lot like asking "What's all the way down?" or "What does everything depend upon?" Back then, I wanted to use what I had learned from tasting the wine of Zen to come up with a connoisseur's answer. But my teacher wouldn't accept my "answers." They were piecemeal answers. Interview after interview, I failed to identify the Source.

In fact, I failed so many times that my teacher gave me the Zen name "Gendo," which means "Source of the Way." The "Way" is Zen. The Way is my life, just as it is, right here and now. So my whole identity, for the rest of my life, was permanently locked in a koan about the Source. I had put my life on top of an imaginary stack of turtles, and now I had no choice but to go deep into Master Panshan's statement "there is nothing at all." And do you know what I found there? I found a red wheelbarrow! I also found white chickens. And a green car with a scratch on the door. And the snood that your Aunt Mabel wore at the fish fry last week.

If you penetrate into the Source, then Panshan's statement "there is nothing at all" comes across in a different way. You may get a glimpse of this by focusing on the word "is," rather than the word "nothing." If you do get a glimpse of the Source, then the implications of Panshan's question, "Where will you find the Mind?" change as well. You discover that the emphasis should be on the word "find," not "Mind." Why? Precisely because you can't find it!

A koan from the collection *The Gateless Gate* puts all of this into more concrete terms. In the koan, we are told that Manjusri Bodhisattva (the archetypal figure of *prajna*, or transcendental wisdom) went to an assembly of the myriad Buddhas of all the Buddha realms. When he arrived, however, he discovered that the assembly was already over! All the Buddhas had returned to their Buddha lands, except for Shakyamuni Buddha and—strangely enough—a girl. The girl was seated to one side of the Buddha, deep in meditation. Seeing this, Manjusri wondered how a human girl could have surpassed the meditative endurance of all those Buddhas. So he asked Shakyamuni about it, and Shakyamuni said, "Why don't you rouse her from meditation and ask her yourself?"

Manjusri snapped his fingers near her. But she didn't wake up. He jumped up and down and carried on, but she remained steadfastly absorbed. He performed all kinds of Bodhisattva magic, but the girl still didn't come out of her meditation. No matter what he did, she remained deeply concentrated.

Puzzled, Manjusri asked Shakyamuni how it could be that he, the great Bodhisattva of Prajna Wisdom, could not bring a simple human girl out of her meditation.

The Buddha said, "I will call forth the Bodhisattva Momyo from the hell realms, and he will show you how it's done."

When Momyo got there, he snapped his fingers just like Manjusri had done, and the girl suddenly opened her eyes! Why do you suppose that a Bodhisattva from hell could do it when Manjusri couldn't? Manjusri is one of the two most important Bodhisattvas in Mahayana Buddhism. Zen meditation halls usually have a statue of him on the altar. He is often depicted riding a lion, and in some cases is shown swinging a flaming sword, ready to lop off your head of delusions. He's a very powerful being and is even considered the teacher of Buddhas. If he is so powerful, so absolutely wise, why was he unable to bring the girl out of meditation? And if Momyo, by contrast, is not nearly at Manjusri's level, how is it he's able to just snap his fingers and effortlessly wake her up? What gives?

Here's something to consider: Manjusri is an expert. He's learned an awful lot. He looks at things with an expert's eye, the eye of one who understands the non-distinction of delusion and enlightenment. So when he snaps his fingers, there really isn't any sound because sound and silence, form and emptiness, are identical. If the girl had come out of her meditation, he wouldn't even have noticed it.

Momyo, on the other hand, is kind of deluded, even though he too is a Bodhisattva, an enlightened being whose sole ambition is the salvation of all other beings. His name means Seed of Delusion. He dwells in the hell realms, suffering alongside the other beings there, trying to save them. For him, there is a world of difference between meditation and non-meditation, delusion and enlightenment. So when he snaps his fingers, there's a loud snap! and the girl wakes up.

Each of these Bodhisattvas, Manjusri and Momyo, can only see things in a certain way. And the way they see things affects the way their lives go. Neither Manjusri nor Momyo has a complete view, just as neither the scientist nor the old woman has a complete view. The scientist is like Manjusri; the old woman is like Momyo. Like I said above, most human beings try to play both ends against the middle, holding on to both views at the same time. But it's also the case that human beings can bridge the gap that stands between these polarized views. Manjusri can't do that. Momyo can't do that. But you can. You, and you alone, can attain the bridge that crosses the abyss that "goes all the way down."

Open to Many Worlds

Like many of his contemporaries, and especially like his friends Ezra Pound and H. D. (Hilda Doolittle), Williams was keenly interested in re-inventing poetry. In making it responsive to the modern world in which he actually lived. He was perhaps a bit jealous, too, when Ezra Pound, his best friend, began to receive acclaim for his two-line poem "In a Station of the Metro" (see "Tapping the Coffin") as well as for numerous other publications that were indebted to East Asian literary traditions. Above all, though, Williams was a man who believed that poetry might—if it could be made to touch life directly and deeply—assuage his desperate need to be appreciated and soothe his profound feelings of loneliness and rejection.

So he turned, in the late 1910s and early 1920s, to the poetry of ancient China. It was there that he learned about the twin traditions of Taoism and Zen.[2] As he searched for models that would help him write the new kind of poetry he wanted to write, he discovered that writing itself was not at all the important thing—you needn't worry about that if you could attain just one glimpse (he used the word frequently) of the authentic reality that lay beyond the patter of social lies. In other words, he became a diva before learning to sing.

The Tang Dynasty poetry that Williams studied was focused on sensory immediacy, a stripped-down simplicity, and avoidance of intrusive, conceptual "explanations." It helped him articulate a primary directive for the composition of poetry, which was "No ideas, but in things." Williams also noticed that Tang poetry focused on ordinary people and objects and that it manifested a kind of equanimity in the face of sorrow, loneliness, and grief. The emphasis on ordinary people and things reflected especially well the value that Williams' placed on his life as a doctor, serving the working class poor of Rutherford, New Jersey. It was amid that sundry, workaday world that Williams said he often experienced a kind of dissolution of the ego that is familiar to anyone who practices meditation. "I lost myself," he wrote, "in the very properties of [my patients'] minds: …I actually became them…. I myself did not exist, nothing of myself affected me." "…when I detached myself from them at the end of a half-hour of intense concentration over some illness which was affecting them, it was as though I were reawakening from a sleep…. I came back to myself…rested."[3]

Crows. Japanese. Pair of six panel screens; ink and gold on paper. Edo period, 1603-1868 (1615–1868), early 17th century. (Seattle Art Museum, Eugene Fuller Memorial Collection. Photo by Seiji Shirono, National Research Institute for Cultural Properties, Tokyo.)

Years after writing "The Red Wheelbarrow," Williams clarified what it was about the literary and visual arts of East Asia that so appealed to him: "They have a museum of Oriental art in Seattle," he wrote, "that presents…one particular painting, or screen, of a hundred crows in flight, nothing more, that might open our minds, were we before it, to many worlds."[4] The screen (it's actually two, six-panel screens of black ink on gold paper) exemplifies the same kind of immediacy and single-pointed focus that characterizes "The Red Wheelbarrow." Like the birds in that screen, the red wheelbarrow consumes the entire sphere of our awareness, leaving "nothing more." It has an immediacy and a palpability that is not undermined by explanation or by references to other things. It is complete like a box and a lid. All you have to do to appreciate it is to stand before it, open to the whole world. Just realize that it's like an old tune that you've been carrying around inside of you since the beginning. If you can't hear it, it's because you're too busy thinking about what it means. But the moment you arrive within the realm of "nothing more," you'll already be singing that song.

What is the meaning of the red wheelbarrow?

If you have to ask, you've already missed it. Just feel the weight of it, the rough handles resting in the palms of your hands, the wheel creaking as it bumps along over the ground, rain water dripping into the grass—and nothing more. If you can do that, then you will already have attained the indispensable bridge that spans the abyss of the world. The ends of that bridge cannot be found, but being right where you are, you will be one acquainted with the Source of it all, whether it's red wheelbarrows, old ladies, turtles, or white chickens all the way down. Then the sound of your rumbling wheelbarrow will thunder throughout the universe.

If you need a little extra help at this point, I humbly suggest that you ask the old lady with the stack of turtles. She really has the *Eye*. Or you could just become, like Williams, a master of the glimpse. It may take twenty or thirty years, but when it happens, the lightning will strike before you have time to cover your ears. Then the thing that's right in front of you will carry the weight of the whole world. It will become your responsibility to help all sentient beings attain the indispensable bridge, to help them follow the path of emancipation. I know it seems like a daunting task. How can you save all beings when you can't even understand an ordinary red wheelbarrow? But right there, you have your answer. Right *here*, you have everything it takes to be a great Bodhisattva, planting the demon seed of nirvana. Just lift up the handles and push on!

> Why does lifting one handle
> Mean that another must be lifted too?
> Who invented this torture device?
> Carrying the whole load, it rolls along
> By itself, the very vehicle of Dharma!

∾

1. Pugliese, Nicholas. "Poet William Carlos Williams' Muse Found, Honored in Rutherford." North-Jersey.com. N.p., 18 July 2015. Web. 28 May 2016.

2. Qian, Zhaoming. *Orientalism and Modernism: The Legacy of China in Pound and Williams*. Durham: Duke University Press Books, 1995. Print.

3. Williams, William Carlos. *The Autobiography of William Carlos Williams*. New York: New Directions, 1967. Print. 356.

4. Ibid. 371.

Outside the Painted Gate

Allen Ginsberg's "First Party at Ken Kesey's with Hell's Angels"

Seeing the world by walking only ridges and tightropes does not make for a good trip. Still, the balancing pole extends everywhere. If you ask me, I'd say just cut off the ends.

First Party at Ken Kesey's with Hell's Angels

Cool black night thru the redwoods
cars parked outside in shade
behind the gate, stars dim above
the ravine, a fire burning by the side
porch and a few tired souls hunched over
in black leather jackets. In the huge
wooden house, a yellow chandelier
at 3AM the blast of loudspeakers
hi-fi Rolling Stones Ray Charles Beatles
Jumping Joe Jackson and twenty youths
dancing to the vibration thru the floor,
a little weed in the bathroom, girls in scarlet
tights, one muscular smooth skinned man
sweating dancing for hours, beer cans
bent littering the yard, a hanged man
sculpture dangling from a high creek branch,
children sleeping softly in their bedroom bunks.
And 4 police cars parked outside the painted
gate, red lights revolving in the leaves.

(1965)

"First Party at Ken Kesey's with Hell's Angels" by Allen Ginsberg (1926–1997) floats in a thin atmosphere of sentence fragments, utterly unconcerned about the need for predication. It is a Polaroid snapshot taken at a party that, now, fifty years later, looks pretty much like the parties of young people today: there is an "us" that declares its rebellious nature with loud music and youthful defiance—and a hovering, interfering "them" that does not like "us." And right there, we have all the ingredients for a lesson in Buddhist ethics—even though "First Party" is hardly more than a list of eye-blinks through the pot smoke. From Ginsberg's perspective, however, there was no need to squeeze a moral meaning out of a party on one night in California in 1965. It was already a sufficiently meaningful symbol of itself.

This was Ginsberg's distinctly Buddhist kind of poetic practice. It was, he explained, "similar to the Dharmic practice of letting go of thoughts [so that you can have] the confidence to observe your own perceptions and discontinuities." By objectively capturing such moments, Ginsberg believed that poetry could be "a ground of purification…." a practice of recognizing that the irretrievable nature of time made it impossible to revise or deny the truth that is evident in every moment.[1]

To see how this works, you may have to spend a little time fluttering Ginsberg's Polaroid snapshot in the quiet air of Zen. But if you patiently wait for its colors to emerge—that is, if you slow down and let the words of "First Party" force you to turn your light inward—then you will find that it becomes a terribly beautiful thing, endlessly unfolding itself within you just as Zen koans do.

Koans are snippets of (usually) ancient masters' dialogs that have become the objects of meditation and realization in the Zen tradition. In koan practice, you begin with a slow, meticulous walk along the tightrope of words, steadily concentrating on each step of the path of language, finding your way to the other side of the intrinsic meaning of the words.

To get at the gist of "First Party at Ken Kesey's," therefore, just slowly and meticulously observe everything in it, step by step, with your mind in a state of graceful, balanced equipoise. When you reach the other side, far beyond the mere dictionary meanings of Ginsberg's words, then you will see the Zen of his poem: that what is important is not the contested territories of right and wrong, or tradition or revolution, but that the origins of human conflict are within you.

Walking Meditation

You are outside. It is a "cool black night" in northern California. You see "cars parked outside in shade / behind the gate," and take note of the unusual idea that shade exists at night. Stars dimly appear "over the ravine." As you approach the house, you notice "a few tired souls hunched over" a fire outside the door. Their "black leather jackets" suggest that these are Hell's Angels, the guardians of the house. At first you think they're there to stop you entering, as though they were the demon sentries of the gated city of Dis, where Dante, horrified, stood and listened to the anguished screams of the damned inside. But it could also be that these sentries are there to prevent those inside the house from getting away.

Inside, the party is rocking. It is three o'clock in the morning, but the lights are blazing and the stereo is blasting. "Twenty youths / [dance] to the vibration thru the floor." The scent of pot is in the air, but it is being discretely smoked in the privacy of the bathroom.

Then, as if you were a disembodied eye, your vision seamlessly returns to the scene outside the house, where crumpled beer cans are "littering the yard," and "a hanged man / sculpture" ominously dangles in a tree. This is followed by another shift such that, from where you stand, you can peer through solid walls to behold "children sleeping softly in their bedroom bunks."

Finally, you go outside again to note the four "police cars parked outside the painted / gate, red lights, revolving in the leaves." You have ended where you began: with cars—the karmic vehicles by which both partyers and party-poopers have all arrived.

If Ginsberg's poem had been a real tightrope, you would have noticed that each step brings with it a little bit of a wobble this way or that way. So it is in with all forms of human walking; it is impossible to move forward without relinquishing some degree of control over your balance. With every step, you risk a fall. When you were a toddler learning to walk, you fell a lot because you didn't yet know how to catch your balance with every step. The same is true in spiritual practice. At first, you stumble and fall, but, gradually, you learn how to respond to the world so that you are constantly able to regain your balance, risking and recovering your stability to make your way. You can spend many years perfecting your understanding of this method by practicing *kinhin*, or walking meditation. And so it is with Ginsberg's poem too. With each step you take, you notice a little wobble here and a little wobble there. These wobbles are nothing that will make you fall out of the poem, but because you're being meticulous about your observations, you notice them.

The main thing that you notice is that this party has drawn the attention of the police. Is "First Party at Ken Kesey's" about youth vs. authority? Freedom vs. control? Hippies vs. pigs? If so, why doesn't Ginsberg give us the arrests, the shouting, the crying, the passive resistance, the billy clubs, and the handcuffs? If you know anything about Ginsberg's life, you know it was all about breaking free of social and political constraints. The tools of his trade were frenzied poetry, drugs, the music of protest, and an anti-materialist, anti-militarist political posture. He was down on The Man. He was not afraid to say so. So why isn't that stuff in his poem? Why is this poem so still and silent in the face of the impending crisis?

Looking again at the poem as a whole, you see that although it has an outside and an inside, there are no real walls or barriers for you—you can float in and out, like a zombie eyeball, going wherever you want, seeing whatever you want.

There is also the specter of authority and the spirit (if not the activity) of revolution. What is the meaning of these two social forces being present together in the poem without contact? And penetrating deeper, what actually is "authority"? Red lights in the trees? (That's all you see of the cops.) What actually is "revolution"? Dancing? (That's all you see of the party-goers.) But is that what you *thought* you saw the first time you read the poem?

To enter the house of this poem is to enter yourself. It is to see that the people in the poem feel that they are either inside or outside, or hovering, fearful, on the margins—and that their different positions on one side or another of their walls and gates is what establishes the sense of their impending conflict. The way Ginsberg has written his poem, however—that is, without explications or judgments—means that you can float through walls and gates and see everything at once. It is as though, for you, there were no inside or outside. Your zombie eye can go wherever it wants to go, and it can occupy, the bodies and lives of anyone in the poem.

Koan practice is often just like this, a matter of seeing things, and people, and statements from multiple, (and sometimes seemingly contradictory) angles. This is the power of zazen, the power to feel around all the contours of your experience with sensitivity and equanimity, sharpening your sense of actualities, instead of reinforcing your attachments by daydreaming.

If you're honest about it, you will recognize all the people in Ginsberg's poem as different aspects of your own life, the different ways that you respond to your experience of the world. Because you are acutely balanced and equanimous, you can see that your own life contains the life experiences of all beings. Your mind is a most amazing thing! When you go deeply enough into the nature of any particular feeling, you discover that all other possible emotions are simultaneously present. Seeing this reveals the complexity of human being. It explains how it is possible that people can be so variable and voluble.

The Buddha, for example, had many different aspects. He was the most radical teacher of personal liberation that ever walked the earth, but he was also the source of the strict rules for monastic behavior. You can dress the Buddha in a blue uniform but he will appear in a tie-dyed shirt. You can braid his hair into a pony tail, but he'll crop it close. You may think he's sprinkling you with daisies, but he'll leave you bleeding on the campus green. Maybe then you think that Ginsberg's poem is all about non-distinction—the "oneness"—of hippies and cops. If that's what you think, then you miss their individual *functions*. On the other hand, if you think one group is irrevocably "inside" and the other group is irrevocably "outside," then you miss the *principle*. If you can't decide either way, then you have to penetrate even deeper into the poem by turning your light inward to see it as your very own life. What do you believe is the cause of conflict within you? How do you respond to conflicting views of politics, sex, religion, drugs, or authority? When people disagree with you, how do you respond? What do you want to be true about the nature of human conflict? What do you *want* the poem to mean?

On and Off the Bus

Of course, Ginsberg's poem emerges from a counter-cultural context in which many groups of people—including Kesey's Merry Pranksters, the Hell's Angels, and establishment politicians—could not sort out their differences. Each group, generally speaking, felt that it was "inside," and that everyone else was "outside." Personally speaking, my instinct is to run with the Merry Pranksters, to think, and take joy, and live in a sense of "togetherness." But if you're walking the tightrope of "togetherness," you eventually discover a whole world of "separation." When it came to the Merry Pranksters and their LSD-fueled magic bus, one was either "on the bus" or "off the bus." You did the scene, including dropping acid, or you didn't. There was no in-between. It was an either-or proposition that perpetuated the conflicts it was meant to resolve.

And let's consider the police. Perhaps you called them because you can't sleep. The music at Kesey's place is too loud, and motorcycles are revving up and down the road. You have to go to work in the morning, and you don't want to be grumpy and groggy-eyed all day. You feel that your freedom to be let alone has been taken away from you. The police, as your representatives, arrive at that noisy house-a-fire to restore your freedom.

Two other groups of people in this poem may likewise be other than they seem. One is the Hell's Angels. They are not quite the same as Kesey or his entourage. They are a group unto themselves. They've been invited to the party, but it's interesting that they cluster around the door instead of (apparently) going in. They are partying with everyone else, but *unlike* everyone else, they do their partying outside, "littering the yard" with beer cans. They occupy a middle ground that is inside the "painted gate," but outside of the house.

The other group of people is hard to see because it is presented so subtly. This group blends in with the revelers, but like the Hell's Angels, they exist in a space of their own that does not participate in either "side" of the imminent confrontation between Kesey and the police. They are the sleeping children.

It might be tempting to think that there is a hopeful message here—that the poem suggests that conflict can be avoided by becoming more like Hell's Angels or sleeping children, groups that occupy a half-way point that is something on the order of compromise. But this is hardly satisfying. The Hell's Angels are just as likely as anyone to have it in for the cops. They have come to the party, but they don't offer any real commitment to their hosts. They want to be included, but fear that they will lose something of their identity by going all "in." They want attention, but will give up nothing to have it. Such people create a kind of protective barrier for themselves, but it is made of self-interest, and will inevitably leave behind a litter of selfishness that others will have to deal with. This may remind you of the nature of addiction. In what ways are you an addict? In what ways do you seek to hide your joneses, pretending that you share an interest with others while furtively seeking to extract a high?

And the children? How in the world are they able to sleep through all the racket? Children do have a remarkable ability to enter the land of Nod. They are sweet and innocent, but they are also oblivious to the conflicts that adults must face. They are blind to what is going on all around them. But I assure you that if you look within, you will find instances of your own denial, places where your need to be safe and secure forced you to close your eyes and sleep through the things that scared you. When I was a sophomore in college, I just hated having to live with a roommate. As well, I wasn't happy with the way things were going academically. So I went to sleep. Even when I couldn't sleep anymore, I often stayed in bed, eyes closed, because I didn't know what to do or how to face my problems. Sleep—even pretended sleep—provided a sense of safety and security—until, that is, a day arrived when the conflicts I was trying to avoid would simply not stop shouting in my ear.

Being in denial like that doesn't always take the form of sleep, however. I remember once, years ago, struggling with the koan "Make this old man stand up without using your hands." I brought response after response to my teacher, but I couldn't pass the koan. I couldn't pass it because I was in denial about something. I couldn't pass it because I wanted to stay blind to something that worried me: what if I fail to help those in need? My teacher at the time was very good about helping me, but it wasn't until I had exhausted all my logical, rational ways of looking at the koan that I was finally able to hear the words of my teacher. I remember the moment well. He said, "You're attached to your own enlightenment." Suddenly, upon hearing those words, I had a great realization. I remember that it seemed in that instant as though everything in the room rushed away from me and all that was left was this wide, open, crystal clear understanding. My eyes had opened and I saw myself as the very thing I had so desperately wanted not to be. Then and there, I helped the old man get up without using my hands.

If you've really investigated every little nook and cranny of Ginsberg's poem, you will be able to see the most important—and perhaps the most subtle—detail about it. It is the fact that what divides you from others and causes conflict, is born of the divisions within you. It is your "inside" and "outside" ideas, your "on the bus" and "not on the bus" ideas, your walls and your gates, your notions of freedom and control, that mean the world can never be at peace. I mean this very literally. World peace, no matter how much you want it, how much good work you do to bring it about, cannot happen until the barriers within are penetrated.

Swinging the Hingeless Gate

What it all comes down to is that gate, that painted gate. It's interesting that this gate is such a seemingly unimportant part of the poem and yet is the literal dividing line between having peace in your life and in the world and suffering both internal and external conflict. As a Buddhist, Ginsberg would not have missed the significance of this gate; it is a terribly important trope in the world of Zen. Gates come up repeatedly in the koan literature, and sometimes we talk about particular teachings and particular sticking points in our practice as "Dharma gates."

The value of the gate metaphor, however, is usually not fully appreciated until we understand how the ancient Chinese progenitors of Zen thought about them. When westerners think of a gate, they think of it mainly as a door—as in a garden gate. In China, however, gates are thought of very differently. They are really thought of as walls, more like imposing barriers, than as doors. Tiananmen, The Gate of Heavenly Peace in Beijing, for example, is actually a massive building comprised

Tiananmen, 1901.

of a platform and a tower that is 216 feet long, 121 feet deep, and 104 feet tall. It's true that there are doors in this "gate," but from the Chinese perspective, Tiananmen is a daunting barrier meant to keep people out.

Given that cultural context, the meaning of *The Gateless Gate*, the title of a collection of koans, is probably a bit clearer. It suggests that the koans initially appear to be (and from an experiential perspective are) barriers. But if you sit with a koan and let it absorb you completely, you begin to see it differently. In concentrating fully on the koan, exploring all of its nooks and crannies, all of its fissures and bumps, all the places where you stick to particular details, it is as though your mind were like sea water, surging in and filling up all the spaces of an underwater cave, taking on its shape. When that happens, the barrier is no longer a barrier. The only barriers are in your mind, or, to continue with the metaphor, the wrong shape of mind.

Zen teaches us to have flexible minds. That way, no matter what our circumstances, no matter what conflicts arise, we can spontaneously respond in exactly the right way. Do you see that this has something to do with freedom and control? The same freedom and control that our hippies and our cops, our Hell's Angels and our sleeping children want? The problem for them all is that they don't know (yet) how to unify the energies of freedom and control. We learn that from the practice of Zen. We learn how to unify freedom and control, so as to resolve any barrier that stands before us.

If you want to resolve barriers between people, it is not enough to go through the door in the gate, waving a white flag. That will do nothing to remove the dividing line between people. The whole barrier must be removed. It is also not enough to get the parties to negotiate a truce because that also does not remove the barrier.

Most people will assume that getting rid of the barrier means doing so physically, as was done when the Berlin Wall was taken down and East and West Germany were re-united. But this response, while symbolically and functionally helpful, still doesn't get rid of the ultimate cause that produces barriers in the first place. Barriers therefore remain—they just take another form. This is why wars cannot be won or lost. The barriers that are physically and politically dismantled "after" a war are just reflections of Mind. It's good to take them down, but if the causes remain, then the physical barriers will eventually be rebuilt, often in another part of the world. So what are you going to do?

You have to enter Ginsberg's painted gate. I don't mean that you pass through the door in the gate. I mean you have to assume the shape of the gate in every way. You have to see the gate within yourself and yourself within the gate. This is an experience that cannot be explained, only pointed to. The figurative language I use to describe the experience—like sea water in an underwater cave, for example—is just that, figurative language. It has nothing to do with the actual experience, which is not imaginative at all; in fact, you could say that it's the opposite of imagination. (See "The Sultan of Savoir" for more about Zen and the limits of the human imagination.) It's a matter of seeing the actual nature of reality.

So you identify with "cars," and "stars," and "ravines." With "souls" and "Hell's Angels" and "one muscular smooth skinned man / sweating dancing for hours." You also have to identify with "a hanged man," with "children sleeping softly in their bedroom bunks," and with the police. When you turn your light inward, you expose yourself to the differences between your view of all these things and the way they really are.

To turn your light inward is to study yourself. When you study yourself, then you and the painted gate of Ginsberg's poem are no longer perceived as two things. There is only "gate." But when there is only "gate," you are gone (or the "you" of your imagination is gone). When you are gone, even though there is only "gate," it is not the gate that you formerly understood. This "gate" is unknown. It is the gateless gate.

To put it another way: All things include all things. It is like a net that has been knotted by the light of numberless, eternal jewels, each reflecting the light of all the others—Indra's Net. Thus, you can say that beyond the painted gate of your mind is a party, but its nature is that of suffering. Beyond the painted gate of your mind, there are rowdy men with guns and drugs, but they just harmless, hungry ghosts that have no place to go. Children sleep in their bunks, but beyond the painted gate of your mind, they are neither innocent nor aware. All of this and more is well within your power to see if you pour yourself into it. It won't be enough to take my word for it. You will have work at it, "sweating dancing for hours," if you will, to the music that is playing in your head. And, then, when at last you tire of the dance, and you go outside into the cool of the evening, you will see, over the dark ravine, the effigy of a hanged man. This too is a painted gate. Beyond it, the hanged man is neither frightening nor morbid, but the manifestation of the nature of all that is at stake in this poem and in your life.

Now I could explain the effigy directly, but that would be to miss the extraordinary similarity it has with a koan from *The Gateless Gate*. It goes like this:

Master Xiangyan Zhixian (?–898) once told his monks, 'It's like a man hanging from the branch of a tree by his teeth, over a deep ravine. His hands are tied behind his back, and his feet cannot reach a single branch. Someone down below calls up to him, begging him to explain the meaning of Zen. If he answers, he loses his life. If he doesn't answer, the questioner loses his. What should he do?'

If you are thinking now about whether it is your own life or the questioner's life that must be sacrificed, then you have not understood the nature of the painted gate, and both you and your questioner will die. What is required to get through this barrier? If you think that it's a matter of going "dead," like the hanged man in Ginsberg's poem, then life will always be a bitter loss for you. If you think it's a matter of dismissing the meaning of Zen, then you might as well sleep your life away. It won't do either to hover just outside the painted gate of this koan, an aloof angel who is afraid to enter hell and afraid to leave it behind. Master Wumen Huikai (1183–1260), the compiler of *The Gateless Gate*, said that working on such koans requires you to swallow them whole. The only problem is that a koan like this is like a hot iron ball. It sticks, burning in your throat. You can neither spit it up, nor gag it down. And yet you must do something—Now! How will you pass through this gate?

Going Beyond the Beyond

One day, long before I had read "First Party at Ken Kesey's," I had had to work on a one-line koan "How do you stop the fighting on the other side of the river?" I always thought of myself as a person of peace, as someone who might willingly take a risk in order to end the suffering of others' disagreements and conflicts. But that koan forced me to acknowledge that I had some pretty serious limitations to what I would be willing to do to "stop the fighting." It's hard work to break down those barriers—and it can hurt, in both the mental and physical sense. By the time peace on the far shore of my life was glimpsed, I had come pretty close to breaking the teacher's collarbone!

Given Ginsberg's enormous sensitivity to the energies of politics and poetry, and given his many decades as a Buddhist, I can only believe that he very much wanted to draw your attention to the painted gate at the end of his poem. He did this in the way that many modern poets do: he broke the second-to-last line of his poem after the word "painted"—not the place that you might think would be most natural—a technique known as *enjambment*. Enjambment causes the reader to land heavily on the first word of the following line, as though it had burst forth from the speaker's mouth with particular emphasis. "Gate." *Gate*. Is there more here than meets the mind's eye? I believe there is.

"Gate" means gate in the ordinary sense, but for many Buddhists it means something else too. When "Gate" is pronounced *gah-tay*), it is the Sanskrit word for "gone." It is part of the great *mantra* (or meditative phrase) that is familiar to every Zen Buddhist in the world, the Prajna Paramita mantra. The mantra reads:

> Gate! Gate! Paragate! Parasamgate!
> Bodhi svaha!

> Gone! Gone! Gone beyond! Gone beyond beyond!
> Hail the awakened one!

A declaration of the state of consciousness of *anuttara-samyak-sambodhi*, or unsurpassed, perfect, complete enlightenment, this mantra is all about the dissolution of barriers, of making gates disappear. The Buddhas that dwell in anuttara-samyak-sambodhi have gone beyond all barriers, passed through all gates, and have even gone beyond their own going. What does it mean to go beyond going beyond?

I have said that Zen is a practice of turning your light inward. When that is your practice, then you'll discover that everything is within you. There is nothing you cannot know and nothing you cannot do. The power to take down walls is one with which each human being is fully endowed. If this were not so, then the absence of power would not exist at all. But it *does* exist; it is important to preserve this absence of power and use it well. You may not understand how the absence of power is able to stop a war, or even to stop the fighting on the other side of the your bed. But if you single-mindedly pursue this question, relinquishing every desire to pose one idea above another, then all the gates of your life will open wide, admitting sentient beings into the light. More simply put, your life will be the gate of your life, hanging in space by its own paint. Now, thinking this over, tell me: How do you go beyond the gate of your life?

> Can you stop the fighting
> On the other side of the world?
> Falling into the dark ravine,
> The way beyond it seems pretty clear.
> Walking home, the hanged man laughs aloud.

1. Johnson, Kent. *Beneath a Single Moon: Buddhism in Contemporary American Poetry*. Shambhala, 2001. Print. 99.

Endless Practice

Light-Years Away From It

Richard Wright's Haiku "810"

Until you are desperate and have nothing else to lose, the light of the morning star will not penetrate Shakyamuni's eye. Still, feeling down about life is no way to master it. Just know that, in approaching the wall, it is easy to make progress. Coming to the edge of the open field at dawn, how can you possibly take a step?

810

> That frozen star there,
> Or this one on the water,—
> Which is more distant?

(1998)

One summer night, when I was about five years old, I woke up to a strange breeze drifting through my bedroom window. I got up and leaned into the frame, inhaling its musty smell. The trees in the neighbor's yard sighed with a hot breath-like air, and a low haze pillowed a galaxy of fireflies. I looked up. Stars glimmered through the leaves like so many little sequins of light, and I was so struck by their beauty that I wanted more than anything to get a closer look at them. I gently uncoupled the hook and eye that kept the screen from flapping on its hinges and pushed it out as far as I could.

The ground outside was about six feet down—not a bad drop for a summer boy of skinned knees and scraped elbows. I squirmed through the opening and let myself fall, the screen window clapping shut above me. Standing in my pajamas, ankle-deep in Lily of the Valley, I felt the cool air moving strangely around and through me. I looked up again to see the stars. Countless millions studded the darkness. Suddenly, I was struck by a feeling that those stars and I were connected. I could not take my eyes off of them because they were looking right through me, a consciousness flowing right into the core of my being. I felt completely exposed, vulnerable, and then terri-fied, in that order. The stars were not evil or menacing, but they had evoked a real-ization that I was not an "I" anymore. Even now, fifty years later, I get goose bumps recalling that night, and the hair on the back of my neck stands up.

The neighbor's teenage son, Perry, had seen me jump out the window. And now he had come over, while at the same time, my mother appeared in the dark window above, probably alerted by the clap of the closing screen. Perry lifted me up. My mother pulled me back into safety, and I felt a relief as of one rescued from a terrible power. I was too young to have understood what had happened to me, but I knew it was important—*more important* than anything I would ever experience again.

Our relationship with the universe can remain just a casual thing until a moment comes when we are in the grips of an experience like that. Until that happens, we inhabit a kind of imaginary space, seemingly at a remove from the rest of reality. Now it may seem like a good idea to get to know that reality better, but, at the same time, we tend to put a lot of distance between ourselves and knowledge of that True Self. We fear it, just as I did that summer night. It's like being exposed to a vision of God. That vision scrapes us clean of the comfortable illusions we have about our separate, solitary, in-control lives. God, in His full grandeur, it is said, does not show himself to human beings because the mere sight of Him would kill us. Thus, God would not reveal himself entirely to Job. Arjuna, the warrior of the epic poem *Bhagavad-Gita*, would have died of the unbearable vision of Krishna's true form had Krishna not quickly resumed a human—albeit blue-skinned—body.

So, when we consider Wright's untitled haiku #810, we can perhaps appreciate why it asks which star is more *distant*—not which is closer. The question is important because it underscores a common theme in our practice: that of the distance between *this* world and that *other* divine world, or world of enlightenment, the world in which Buddhas dwell. It places before us a "here" and a "there," the same "here" and "there" faced by Job and Arjuna. It is a space so vast that we fear we will lose our lives if we close the gap between ourselves and the True Self. Yet, to remain here, in the realm of our suffering, is not much of a life either. Thus, if you want to take up the Zen path, you had better get comfortable with the discouragements and doubts of being stuck between "here" and "there."

As a college professor, I see students every day who cannot write. They believe they *ought* to be able to: after all, they've been using words to think and to speak for many years. Yet the sheet of paper in front of them remains implacable. It stretch-es away from them like a Greenland of undisturbed snow. They sit frozen, pen un-capped, waiting painfully for the words to come. If you were to ask them which essay is "more distant"—the one they're writing now (in a halting sort of way), or the one that they will turn in next Friday at 5:00 PM—they will tell you that the ideal is near and the real is far.

Though their hands are on the paper, and their eyes are fixed to the words that are scribbled there, it is nevertheless that miserable sheet that is "more distant" than the finished, "grade-A" product that flutters in their minds, out of reach. It is a paradox that engenders such thorough-going discouragement that to take even a single step into the virgin snow of their notebooks is tantamount to failure.

I feel for them. Who doesn't place the ideal before the real? When you were a kid in the back seat of the family car, you probably asked your parents, "Are we there yet?" If your parents said, "Not yet," what you probably heard was, "We're light-years away from it!" Then, you and your sibling began to poke and shove one another, a pastime developed to cope with discouragement. If you're a parent whose kids ask, "Are we there yet?" you know—*you know* you're doomed. Anything you say that is remotely truthful won't staunch the feeling of bored discouragement in the back seat. You reach for ameliorating words. You gingerly offer the vaguely encouraging "Almost" and then you brace for impact.

When we know a great distance divides our "here" from our "there," discouragement is sure to follow. It's no surprise, then, that stories about discouragement are quite common in our tradition. In one famous example, the Buddha's own monks became discouraged when he had left them alone to meditate on impermanence in a charnel ground. Meditation on death is not supposed to be merely morbid. Rather, it is meant to dispel the deluded view that ego can somehow escape the law of impermanence if it accumulates wealth, a superior social position, and fame. But, surrounded by corpses in various states of disintegration and having no teacher to rely upon, the monks began to feel that awakening was surely so far away that it would be futile to seek it. So they gave up—permanently—by committing suicide.

The Zen tradition too has a take on the nature of discouragement as is reflected in the awakening experience of Huiming. Huiming was one of several hundred monks who studied under the Fifth Zen Patriarch, Hongren Daman (601–674). The story goes that, in the middle of the night, Hongren secretly transmitted the Dharma to an illiterate young man who worked as an assistant in the monastery kitchen. This young man, Huineng Dajian (638–713), had only been in the monastery for about eight months. As one from southern China, he was presumed to be culturally and spiritually naive, completely unworthy of being the successor of any teacher, let alone the successor of the Fifth Patriarch. Assigned to hull rice, he had never even been inside the Dharma hall. Hongren alone recognized Huineng's extraordinary understanding of the Dharma and wished to make Huineng his heir. Fearing that his monks would react badly (perhaps even violently) to his choice, Hongren conferred succession upon Huineng in the middle of the night, while everyone else was asleep. He then helped Huineng slip out of the monastery unseen. He instructed Huineng to cross the river, and to run for his life back to southern China, where he was to remain in hiding for a period of years until it was safe to reveal his identity as the Sixth Zen Patriarch.

At the monastery the following morning, and for several days thereafter, it was business as usual. The only thing that seemed different to the monks was that Hongren was no longer delivering talks. Eventually, the monks also noticed that the illiterate rice-huller had disappeared. Putting two and two together, the monks realized that Hongren had given the robe and the bowl of Dharma succession to a most unworthy being. So they set out *en masse* to search for Huineng, firmly resolved to retrieve the robe of succession, by force, if necessary.

This is where Huiming comes into the story. Huiming had been a general in the military before becoming one of Hongren's monks. He had the skills to track Huineng, even though Huineng had a head start of several days. Eventually, Huiming and the angry, jealous monks cornered Huineng in the Dayu Mountains. The jig was up, and Huineng knew it. He said to Huiming, "The robe and bowl are just symbols of the faith. Why fight over them?" Then he placed the robe of succession on a rock and bade Huiming to take it.

Huiming was in an exhausted, frustrated, and discouraged state of mind. He had secretly wanted that robe very much, and he was very distressed that he had not won the Fifth's Patriarch's favor. But when he tried to lift the robe, he couldn't do it. It was as though the robe were fused to the rock.

At just that moment, Huiming's loss of the robe, and, more importantly, his own failure to have awakened himself, overcame him. His whole world, and the precious thing he had worked for, the thing that he had struggled years to be worthy of, or even to obtain by theft, had slipped through his fingers forever. Shaking and sweating with this realization, his ego shattered, he said, "I have come for the teaching, not for the robe."

Huineng replied, "Not thinking good, not thinking evil, what is your original face before your parents were born?"

When Huiming heard those words, they went right into him, through him, in a most intimate way. The "story" he had been telling himself about who he was, about what the Dharma is, was no longer there to protect him from that one, ego-killing question. And, *bang!* just like that, he experienced a great enlightenment.

It's important to understand the circumstances that led to Huiming's awakening. It's important to see that it happened because his feelings of frustration, disappointment, failure, and discouragement had completely dissolved a deluded thought that he had been carrying around in his heart for a very long time: belief in a "here" that is more distant than the "there" of awakening. You could say instead that he fundamentally *disbelieved* that this world, right here and now, is the self-same world of perfect awakening. It was his fundamental *doubt* that prevented him from seeing the truth that was right under his nose. When that doubt died, Huiming was born.

The hard part of this, of course, is that relinquishing your doubt usually means you must suffer some pretty awful discouragement first. Doubt often arises when you hear about the Buddha's incredibly hard work to attain enlightenment. You wonder whether you have what it takes to really emulate his effort to save all sentient beings from old age, sickness, and death. How are you going to do that while you take out the garbage, or ask your boss for a raise, or change a dirty diaper? How do you do that as a political refugee or the bereaved parent of a dead child? Even if you are undaunted by the challenge and set out with confidence to cross your spiritual miles, you will eventually find out just how impossible it is to get to the "far shore" of nirvana. In fact, what you discover is even more discouraging than the matter of great distance. You discover that the farther you go, the farther you have to go.

It's exactly like the story of Mazu Daoyi (709–788), who was sitting zazen one day when master Nanyue Huairang (677–744) happened by and asked him what he was doing.

"I'm sitting zazen to become a Buddha," said Mazu.

Huairang picked up a piece of a tile and sat down, rubbing it. After a while, Mazu said, "What are you doing?"

Huairang replied, "I'm polishing this tile to make it a mirror."

"How can you make a mirror by polishing a tile?"

Huairang said, "If I can't make a mirror by polishing a tile, how can you become a Buddha by sitting zazen?"

The point, of course, is that we already have Buddha-nature. That means that trying to acquire it is like looking for a light with a lamp. It seems ridiculous, but that's what we do. We go on an endless journey in search of something we'll never find because it isn't external to our lives. The futility of all that eventually becomes immensely painful, leading to terrible feelings of discouragement.

If we aren't terribly clear about how we are already living a perfect, whole, and complete life *right here, right now*, with all of our impulses toward greed, anger, and foolishness, then it's pretty easy to conclude that we are too thick, too insensitive, too spiritually ungifted to realize what purportedly is right under our noses. It is only a short step from there to making the mistake of thinking some people just have a knack for awakening, and some don't. I have watched, helpless to do anything, as that kind of unhealthy attitude devoured a friend and left nothing behind but blame and sour grapes.

But if discouragement is unavoidable (and I think it is), you can avoid being up-ended by it altogether with the help of a good teacher. A good teacher can help you contextualize your feelings of discouragement, desperation, and outright failure. Such help is indispensable for stabilizing your practice and helping you to see that discouragement actually has a positive side. When you see your discouragement in this way, you realize that it is just the shadow of faith.

And the greater your faith, the greater your discouragement, when it comes. It's just like the writing student who can't see that her own mind is already perfect, whole, and complete just the way it is. So she's stuck. She has to write to succeed, but she thinks only of the finished work that doesn't yet exist, missing entirely that everything she needs and wants is right at her fingertips.

Until you are driven to desperation by the search for enlightenment, awakening will simply not happen. I'm not saying that you need to feel down about life in order to master it. I'm saying that thoroughly silencing your doubts about the unity of enlightenment and delusion, or about the Buddha and sentient beings, or about the nearness or the distance of nirvana's star means coming to the point at which you have nothing left to lose. The robe of succession is already yours. It is not a thing you can chase, track down, and conquer. You're wearing the robe now, even if you don't recognize it. It is the birthright of all sentient beings.

So when you read Wright's poem with that frame of mind, you may perhaps realize that, like Huiming, you too have been carrying around a belief that this life is not the real life you are supposed to be living. You may believe that if you struggle long enough, and travel far enough, you will discover a way to move from suffering to joy. But is that how the spiritual journey really works?

To answer that question, you need to do a lot of sitting. Sitting in meditation develops *joriki*, or concentration power. When your concentration power is well developed, you are able temporarily to suppress the cravings and aversions that muddy the mind. The initial result of this is that you behave with greater awareness and equanimity, benefitting your health, reducing your stress, and clarifying your moral values. It also does something all-important: it prepares your mind for the moment of awakening.

Using a metaphor that is strikingly similar to Wright's, Hakuun Yasutani Roshi (1885–1973) explains it this way:

> ...we can say that the mind of a Buddha is like water that is calm, deep, and crystal clear, and upon which the moon of truth reflects fully and perfectly. The mind of the ordinary man, on the other hand, is like murky water, constantly being churned by the gales of delusive thought and no longer able to reflect the moon of truth. The moon nonetheless shines steadily upon the waves.... It is imperative, therefore, that [the gales of delusive thought] be stilled. Once they abate, the waves subside, the muddiness clears, and

we perceive directly that the moon of truth has never ceased shining. The moment of such realization is *kensho*, i.e., enlightenment.[1]

When I first read those lines in 1978, I was ready to sign up for the long trek to *kensho*; I was convinced that if I tried hard I could get there. But what strikes me now, decades later, is the notion that the moon (or a star) never ceases shining. I'm not speaking of the merely scientific fact that somewhere above the clouds the sun is always shining. I'm not merely stating that stars shine even in the middle of the day. I am saying that the light of the moon, or the morning star, or the evening star, or for that matter *the back porch light that you turned off yesterday* is shining now, everywhere, as surely as you are breathing and reading this book.

But I didn't get there by sitting zazen alone. When I say that meditation serves to prepare the mind for awakening, what I mean is that zazen prepares your mind to handle a moment of magnified desperation. A moment in which you are completely gutted, hollowed out by the failure to reach your star, the failure to seize the robe of awakening by force.

More than 2500 years ago, Siddhartha attained enlightenment under exactly the same circumstances. It is said that he attained enlightenment as he glimpsed the light of the morning star. But that star was just the trigger. Siddhartha's mind had first been prepared for several years to be able to respond as it did to his own limitations of mind—with equanimity. But there was also his desperation. We don't usually think of the Buddha as desperate, but what else would you call his abandonment of wife and child, his abandonment of his spiritual friends, and even his abandonment of the spiritual traditions to which he had devoted his life? On top of it all, there was his dramatic, almost frightening ultimatum to himself to never get up from his meditation seat under the Bodhi tree until he had fully resolved the great matter of life and death. It was do or die.

That desperation, that feeling that all has been lost, that everything you ever believed to be true about yourself has failed to help you resolve your doubts, must circulate through your meditative awareness for many long years. By repeatedly doing this, repeatedly confronting your fantasies about who you are, will put you in a position to be triggered by even the slightest jolt of experience. Sometimes, as with Huiming, it is the words of a teacher that provide that jolt.

For the great master Xiangyan Zhixian (?–898), it was the sound of a pebble striking the woody base of a stalk of bamboo. It could be the cry of bird at dawn, or the sight of curtains blowing in an open window. For me, it was the act of pulling my shoelace tight. Whatever it is, that little jolt lights up the hollowness of our failure with an overwhelming brilliance. Suddenly, the real is understood to be neither distant nor near, but *here. Now. Unborn. Everlasting.*

For the Buddha, that trigger was a glimpse of the morning star. At just that moment, in a response that emanated out of everything that he had suffered and endured to prepare for it, he realized the truth and declared, "I and all beings on earth together attain enlightenment at the same time." It is an amazing statement. It wasn't just one of those adolescent, gee-whiz moments when you discover a new thought about yourself. His statement was what we call the "lion's roar," a claim that is irrefutably authentic, rare, wondrous.

To be able to say such a thing without pretense is inconceivably rare. We should not say such a thing ourselves unless we have eradicated every shadow of a doubt about who we really are. It's not the same as *believing*. Believing is what puts beautiful stars out of reach in heaven and useless mirages in the puddles at our feet. But there is more to it than that. Believing—*faith*—is necessary too.

When you have faith that the Buddha's enlightenment was not just his own but all beings', you find the basis for genuine practice—which is also the means by which you abnegate the distance between suffering "here" and awakening "there." It was Richard Wright's faith that balanced the extraordinary discouragement he endured in the last 18 months of his life. Suffering a terminal illness and grieving the loss of cherished friends and his mother, Wright sustained himself by composing *over 4,000 haiku*—a life's work that was the capstone of his career. It was an activity born of abiding faith that was itself born of great discouragement.

Buddhist faith can take you beyond all conceptions of delusion and enlightenment, beyond all dualities of body and mind and the bodies and minds of others. This faith is the light of emancipation that covers the world and washes the sky. And this great light is none other than your own life, just as it is.

Is this just a kind of devotional exaggeration? If you think so, you're missing the mark. If you're not sure, you still have several light-years to travel before you get to the star that is shining in the puddle at your feet. If you conceive a link between Shakyamuni Buddha and all the beings that were crawling, swimming, walking, or flying through the world at the time of his awakening, even *that* does not reach the great matter of life and death. It is not a link like that.

If you truly want to understand Shakyamuni Buddha's lion's roar, then you too must glimpse the morning star at dawn. I am not referring to the morning star that you locate on the star map or find in the sky. I mean the star that you lit before you were born. Don't think of the star as outside of yourself, even though you are drenched in its light. You cannot see this star apart from seeing anything. But to say that the star is "everything" is still not understanding. Look closely at what the great master Keizan Jokin (1268–1325) said:

If you want an intimate understanding of enlightenment, you should get rid of "you" and "Gautama" at once and quickly understand this matter of "I." "I" is the great earth and beings as "and." "And" is not "I" as the old fellow Siddhartha. Examine carefully, deliberate carefully, and clarify this "I" and this "and." Even if you clarify the meaning of "I," but you fail to clarify "and," you lose the discerning eye.[2]

"I" means Shakyamuni Buddha realizing himself as all beings and all beings realizing themselves as Shakyamuni Buddha. "And" means Shakyamuni Buddha realizing Shakyamuni Buddha, all beings realizing all beings, and the morning star realizing the morning star. If Keizan had been able to read Wright's poem, he might have written, *Clarify this "star" and this "or." Even if you clarify "star," failing to clarify "or" will cost you the discerning eye.*

What is that "discerning eye" of which Keizan speaks? Do you have it? If you don't have it, can you get it? If you do have it, can you see through it? Can you, like Shakyamuni Buddha, say what it is you see with it? The discerning eye is the eye that sees which star is "more distant." It is not different from the eye in your own head, which is Shakyamuni's eye. Again, master Keizan explains: "However immensely diverse the mountains, rivers, land, and all forms and appearances may be, all of them are in the eye of the Buddha. And...the eye has become you. Buddha's eye has become everyone's whole body, each standing tall."[3]

"The eye has become you" means that "that frozen star there" and "this one in the water" see you. All beings throughout time and space see you now. But if you cannot see them seeing you, it is only because you still believe that you are an ordinary person and that Buddha is a Buddha. You may search until the end of time, but you will never become a Buddha if this is how you think. Still, you must not forget this: the search you are on, the search that leaves you empty-handed again and again, the search that leads ineluctably to the pain of never being able to lift the robe of transmission is none other than the moment of Shakyamuni Buddha glimpsing the morning star at dawn.

When you come upon that moment, down to the point of desperation, when you are backed into the corner of your own mind, then and only then, does the kalpa fire that destroys the universe go raging through your life, incinerating every cherished opinion, every sacred belief that is holding you back. Painful as it may have been, your life is about to change. You behold the formless catastrophe of your life and know that, even now, there is a failure. The difference, though, is that this failure to reach across the light-years of your being is only a failure to believe your own delusions. Like a star in the daylight, the emancipation of your life is immediate and universal. It consumes the entire sky, leaving nothing out, saving all sentient beings.

It is hard to see
the stars at noon: But tell me:
Not thinking "here" or "there,"
What was the gleam in Buddha's eye
Before God said, "Let there be light"?

1   Roshi, Philip Kapleau. *The Three Pillars of Zen: Teaching, Practice, and Enlightenment.* 19th printing. Boston: Beacon, 1965. Print. Beacon Religion 242. 29.

2   Keizan, Zen M. *Transmission of Light (Denkoroku): Zen in the Art of Enlightenment.* Trans. Thomas Cleary. San Francisco: North Point Press, 1990. Print. 4.

3   Ibid.

The Far Shore

Walt Whitman's
"Facing West from California's Shores"

Striding forward, it leaps away. Holding still, it lingers in the distance.
Still, one horse on the merry-go-round is in the lead. How can you close the gap?

Facing West From California's Shores

Facing west from California's shores,
Inquiring, tireless, seeking what is yet unfound,
I, a child, very old, over waves, towards the house of maternity,
       the land of migrations, look afar,
Look off the shores of my Western sea, the circle almost circled;
For starting westward from Hindustan, from the vales of Kashmere,
From Asia, from the north, from the God, the sage, and the hero,
From the south, from the flowery peninsulas and the spice islands,
Long having wander'd since, round the earth having wander'd,
Now I face home again, very pleas'd and joyous,
(But where is what I started for so long ago?
And why is it yet unfound?)

(1867)

"Facing West from California's Shores" by Walt Whitman (1819–1892) presents the spiritual search as a circular path around the globe. It was a journey which, Whitman believed, had begun in antiquity in "Hindustan," and it would end there too, in both a literal and figurative sense, the human race returned at last to the arms of Mother India.

From our perspective today, circumnavigation of the Earth as a geo-spiritual "manifest destiny" seems naively ignorant of certain political and cultural realities.

Yet Whitman was neither the only, nor the most recent, American poet to think of the United States as the last leg of humanity's triumphal westward migration around the globe. Traces of such thinking can be found in the work of writers as diverse as Amy Lowell, William Carlos Williams, Robinson Jeffers, and Gary Snyder. But even when Whitman's "circle almost circled" is viewed strictly as a metaphor, it bears a remarkable similarity to the Zen symbol that everyone has seen: the *enso*, a circle traditionally painted with ink and brush.

The resemblance between these circles is not just a matter of circularity. The

Enso, or Zen circle.
Painting by John Gendo Wolff.

enso is almost always painted with a gap between its "head" and its "tail," a blank space that corresponds to Whitman's "Western sea," the Pacific Ocean. And therein lies the problem: crossing that ocean is not so easy to do. In fact, it is so difficult, and the destination so remote, that Whitman's persona has grown old trying to get there. Likewise, "the far shore" of nirvana is so distant that, even if you spent many thousands of lives trying to get there, you might still be "seeking what is yet unfound" for a very long time.

To come so close, yet be so far from the goal of awakening is the message of Whitman's poem. It reminds me of one of the so-called *nanto*, or "difficult," koans of the Zen tradition in which master Wuzu Fayan (1024–1104) tells his students that the practice of Zen is like a buffalo trying to pass through a lattice window—a very strange image! The head, horns, body, and hooves of this buffalo, Wuzu explained, have all passed through the lattice window, but for some reason the tail cannot pass. Why can't it pass? If a buffalo can get its whole body through the window, why can't it get its little, tiny tail through?

You could spend years on this koan and never pass it. But even if you can't pass it, it's still clear what it is all about: every step we take on the path to enlightenment seems but half the distance of the step before. If you know anything about mathematics, you know this means that you will always continue to make progress, but that you will also never get to the end of your journey. Hearing this, who wouldn't despair?

It would seem as though practice is meant to bring you tantalizingly close to the goal but let you down in the end. But do you really have to be contented with this? Perhaps not. My first *sesshin*, or multi-day retreat, with my teacher, Myoyu Roshi, was a wonderful experience, but several months passed before I saw her again at another sesshin. When I thought about this "gap" in our contact with one another,

I remembered an image I had seen at Mt. Tremper, New York, where Daido Loori Roshi used to teach. It was an image of an enso, but the enso didn't have a gap. Above it were the words, "No gap!"

So at this second sesshin, I asked Myoyu Roshi about this.

"At the Mountains and Rivers Order Temple," I said, "they teach 'No gap!' What do you teach?"

Without a moment's hesitation, she said, "It's so wonderful to see you again."

Does this help you understand that gap a little better? Myoyu Roshi's answer seems so easy, so effortless. And it was. But that effortlessness was the result of decades of accumulated practice experience. She worked incredibly hard to arrive at a place where she could wield the heavy sword of taking and giving life without any struggle at all.

The rest of us, of course, must struggle mightily. This is what Whitman is getting at when he describes his long, long journey, "starting westward from Hindustan, from the vales of Kashmere, / From Asia, from the north, from the God, the sage, and the hero, / From the south, from the flowery peninsulas and the spice islands." It has been an exhausting trip just to be able to "look afar" "over waves" to the primordial source of being. I see him, "Long having wander'd since, round the earth having wander'd," bent with age, his white beard fluttering in the breeze near the shore of Monterey.

Yet this persona of Whitman's is still "Inquiring, tireless, seeking what is yet unfound." Where does he come up with all that energy? How does he remain inspired? This aspect of the path also reminds me of my teacher. She had more juice as a 60-year-old woman than I've seen in many 20-somethings! No one could keep up with her! She put forth ceaseless effort to make the Dharma available to anyone who was interested. She sacrificed personal time, personal space, and material things so that the wisdom and compassion of Buddhism could be passed on. When it came to putting forth effort, Myoyu Roshi gave 100 percent all the time. She often reminded us that this kind of practice effort, known as *virya-paramita*, or the "perfection of effort," is one of the six (sometimes ten) paramitas, ideals toward which we should strive. Virya-paramita, Roshi would tell us, is mentioned more often, by far, than any of the other paramitas in Buddhist scripture.

If you want to close that gap, then, you have to work very hard. In the face of such a daunting spiritual practice, you have to be willing to exert an iron kind of resolve to have any hope of reaching the far shore that is enlightenment. Any reading of ancient Zen texts will confirm this. Our Ancestor Teachers consistently advocated such iron resolve. This is not because they were zealots who knew no limits, but because the path is a circle—and that means it's endless.

What kind of resolve is this? Is it a matter of surviving a sesshin? Is it just life-long practice? Is it sitting zazen every day in a routine way? I once had a teacher (not Myoyu

Roshi) who said that having 50 percent resolve won't get you there. Even 80 or 90 percent resolve won't get you there. Only 100 percent effort is effective. You could practice 10,000 years, putting forth 99.9 percent effort, and you will have wasted your time. You might think that's an exaggeration, but I'd wager that giving 100 percent effort will only get you to a place where, like the speaker of Whitman's poem, all you can do is wistfully "look afar" at a destination that is still just out of reach. It's like "rounding third" in baseball, except that home plate is infinitely far away.

In Case 9 of *The Gateless Gate*, a monk asked master Xingyang Qingrang (830–888), "Great-Penetration-Into-Perfect-Wisdom Buddha sat in zazen for ten *kalpas* and could not attain Buddhahood. He did not become a Buddha. How could this be?"

Xingyang said, "Your question is self-explanatory."

"But he sat zazen for thousands of years! Why could he not attain Buddhahood?" asked the monk, perplexed.

"Xingyang replied, "Because he could not become a Buddha."

In thinking about this, you might wonder whether you're cut out for Zen. Do you have the resolve to sit for ten kalpas? A *kalpa* is a classical Indian unit of time that is almost incalculably long. It has been said that a kalpa is the amount of time it would take an angel to wear away a block of stone one cubic mile in size by brushing its wing against it once every 100 years. And the Buddha of this koan sat for *ten* kalpas! If *a Buddha* puts in that much effort and still can't close the gap and become a Buddha, what are *your* chances of doing so?

You may be happy to learn that your chances are actually pretty good. I know this because I know something about Whitman's life that perhaps you do not know: he was never in California. He did not spend one nanosecond of his life on the shore of the Eureka State. But he could write effortlessly about it, just as if he had lived there.

How was Whitman able to transcend geography with such ease? How does Myoyu Roshi just effortlessly lift the iron yoke of teaching? The clue is in the poem. Whitman appears as "very old," a white-bearded, "father Christmas" sort of figure standing on a beach. But he also appears as "a child." Like my teacher, he has an open, wondering, innocent, and loving perspective—the joyful perspective of childhood that can make even a crack in the ceiling or the sound of a creaky garden gate seem exquisitely beautiful. Such illuminations are the magic that allow us to go wherever we want to go, to do whatever we want to do.

But you can't just pretend to be a kid. You can act like a Zen idiot all you want to, but that's not going to get you to the far shore. It's not going to close that gap. That kind of openness and joy arise as a result of many years of practice, of "long having wander'd...round the earth...." Specifically, that kind of willing openness to see your life as anything you want it to be comes from realizing that nirvana is *samsara*, the delusive churning of our minds. The trouble is, however, that that realization comes only from understanding clearly that the reverse is also true: samsara is nirvana.

And that means that the Zen path is one of pitting your supreme personal resolve for enlightenment against the seemingly irresolvable source of delusion. It is to face, day in and day out, year after year, the fact that, with every insight, every "success" in your practice, there are ever subtler forms of attachment. It means that for every cure, there is a sickness. When all is said and done, It isn't said, and It isn't done. Practice goes on and on, without end. The path remains a "circle almost circled."

So when you take up your staff and head out to cross the mountains and rivers of your life, you may believe that you will reach your destination. And why shouldn't you? You have been told, over and over, that you have Buddha-nature. As you travel, you gradually become aware that the destination is much farther away than you thought. Yet you don't give up because you are now so far along that you think you might as well keep going. Years pass. Then decades. And you're still not "there." You're more relaxed and self-accepting than you ever were, but the longing to close the gap remains.

On one December night several years ago, a group of students came to Myoshinji for the *Rohatsu* sesshin, which traditionally culminates on the anniversary of the Buddha's enlightenment (December 8, in the Zen tradition). But there was a blizzard that night, and we couldn't get our cars up the long, steep driveway to the temple. It was dark. It was snowing so hard that we couldn't see where we were driving. We tried everything we could think of to get our cars up that hill—chains—logs—putting strips of old carpeting under our tires—but nothing worked. Whatever we did, we got stuck, went into the ditch, blocked the driveway, or were dangerously trapped on the highway. Later, during the retreat, the matter came up in one of Myoyu Roshi's talks. She said, "The temple *should* be hard to get to."

Just writing those words makes my throat swell and my stomach crush itself into a ball. I shake with tears. *The temple is hard to get to.* Sure, anyone can *drive* to Myoshinji. But who, in the end, will get up the hill? So close, and yet so far, how is it that that silly little gap in our circle is so hard—so *monstrously* hard, to close? Why is it that the tail of the buffalo cannot pass through the lattice window? Because samsara and nirvana are one and the same. It is what makes our path endless, and it is also the means by which we can close the gap.

Which tells you something: there must be another way of looking at the path—its nature, the effort required to complete it, and whether you'll make it in the end. Having this other view can help you avoid being crushed by discouragement.

Did you notice that Whitman ends his poem with a parenthetical statement? Frankly, that's kind of a weird thing to do in poetry. It just kind of hangs there at the end of the poem like the tail of Wuzu's buffalo. If you think about it, the poem is like a lattice window. Why won't this window admit Whitman's last questions, the little tail of "Where is what I started for so long ago? / And why is it yet unfound?"

The point I'm making here is that if you see Whitman's looking for something that is "yet unfound" as a problem, *that* is your problem. *That* is why you can't close the gap or pass your tail through the window. When you see the inexhaustible nature of your self-clinging and want to rid yourself of it, once and for all, you can't do it. But you're seeing something as a problem that is not a problem at all. And the reason you don't recognize this is because you have come so far, so very far.

Stuck at this point on the path, some teachers will tell you that there is no such thing as enlightenment. If you ever hear those words, don't listen to them. Run away as fast as you can! Such teachers are confused. Enlightenment is real.

It's just that it's not a "thing."

When you think that what you're missing is a problem, then you can't close the gap. It opens before you as vast as the whole Pacific Ocean. It's so wide you can't swim across it. When the gap is a problem, it's because innocence and experience are divided. It's because you see a circle with a gap in it. Somewhere, way out there, on the edge of the ego's continent, you have to find a little Zen magic that will change all of this. Now I suppose you will want me to tell you what that little thing that changes everything is—and I will—but first, just for a moment, I want you to put yourself in Whitman's big, soggy boots.

Whitman was a guy who trumpeted all kinds of hip-swaggering, sledge-slinging, bawdy-song-singing, out-of-doors-fucking, self-celebration in his poetry. But he was in fact incredibly fearful of human contact. He probably spent most of his life in frustrated, unwished-for celibacy. He probably did not mingle with the "toughs and the beards" as the persona of some of his more famous poetry suggests. In some sense, Whitman was a failed human being. As he grew older, he began to suffer from delusions of grandeur, thinking of his poetry as a kind of "scripture" that ought to be read each day by worshipful admirers.

Yet Whitman is nevertheless America's great poet, our national treasure (if we had such things). And he *was* great because he accepted his mind. He accepted it so thoroughly that, for him, there was no difference at all between real places in the world and the places in the universe of his cosmic mind. Can you, like Whitman, adopt that mind? Can you, like Whitman, be "a child, very old"? Can you harmonize beginner's mind—the mind that looks at everything with fresh, child-like eyes—with the mind of wisdom? In fact, can you do Whitman one better and see the identity of innocence and experience?

When we have most certainly failed because, out of desperation, we must be what we must be, the little bit of Zen magic that changes everything is that we just relax. We just stop trying so hard to be wise. Instead of trying to close the gap, we just give up and let our minds be. And isn't that where we began so long ago—so long ago, when we were children, letting our minds be whatever we wanted them to be?

You see, closing the gap in the circle is a matter of taking just one more little step toward wisdom—but it's a little step *backward* that brings you all the way home, all the way back to the place you started from so long ago. That little step backward is to just not know. This is not the same as being ignorant or going into a trance or hiding in denial. Not knowing is vast like the sky or vast like the Pacific Ocean. Not knowing means that enlightenment is always "yet unfound." If you think you've found enlightenment, you haven't. That's when the "yet unfound" is a lattice window or a gap in the circle. But when you just let the "yet unfound" be what it is, then the lattice window disappears, and so does the circle. All that remains is an infinite and wondrous gap. Then innocence and experience become the very same thing, like Whitman's very old child. Then everything is fresh and beautiful, everything is precisely and exquisitely perfect—as when you were young and could sit quietly, without worry, listening to the mourning doves cooing in the eaves, or watching a dragonfly as it hovered above your bare feet.

When you take that little step backward, then everything is exactly as it should be. No hindrances arise. Sunlight melts among the red leaves of the barberry. Rain falls into the lake. I hope that I can meet you there someday, like an old friend, strolling along the same beach, exclaiming, "How wonderful! How wonderful it is to see you again!"

> An ancient child walking backward
> Over the ocean of life and death
> Clearly sees the unobstructed Way.
> Amid the open window of my house,
> Dandelions bloom and a thousand starlings swirl.

Index

CPSIA information can be obtained
at www.ICGtesting.com
Printed in the USA
LVOW11s0345290917
550089LV00001B/10/P